Lyubov Belozerskaya-Bulgakova
MY LIFE WITH MIKHAIL BULGAKOV

TRANSLATED BY Margareta Thompson

Ardis, Ann Arbor

Copyright © 1983 by Ardis

Ardis Publishers
2901 Heatherway
Ann Arbor, Michigan 48104

All rights reserved. No part of this publication may be reproduced, stored in a retrieval system or transmitted in any form or by any means without the written permission of the publisher.

Translated from the Russian, L. E. Belozerskaya-Bulgakova, O med vospominanii.

ISBN 0-88233-433-6
ISBN 0-88233-434-4

CONTENTS

Getting Acquainted 7

In the Dovecot 16

At the Lyamins' 31

Koktebel—The Crimea 35

No. 4 Maly Levshinsky Street 47

Our Last Nest 67

Some Thoughts about the Theater of Those Years 117

GETTING ACQUAINTED

Moscow had just noisily celebrated the New Year of 1924. At that time the city had an abundance of all kinds of food and the ruble was holding steady... A group of the "Changing Landmarks" people had returned to their country from Berlin. Some of them wanted to get to know, or at least to meet, Muscovite writers and journalists. An evening party was arranged at a luxurious private house on Denezhny Lane. I was present at that party.

There were three of them who came together: Dmitry Stonov, Yury Slezkin and Mikhail Bulgakov. They should be remembered separately, and not as the three musketeers. The first one, I remember, wrote stories and was published often in those days. And then there was Yury Slezkin. Was it really that same Petersburg-Petrograd darling whose successes with women were legendary? He was nice-looking, with dark hair, lively black eyes, and a birthmark on his cheek which was meant for the destruction of female hearts... Only his mouth was not nice; it was cruel, almost frog-like. He was the author of the celebrated novel *Olga Org*. The corners of his heroine's mouth drooped like an "inverted new moon," and the girls all went crazy making sour faces so that they'd look like inverted new moons. The novel was tragic and was reprinted many times after 1915, and if my memory does not fail me a movie, *Burnt (Scorched?) Wings* was made from it. The ballerina Coralli played the main role. Everyone sobbed.

Sometimes Yury Slezkin wrote under the pseudonym Georges de Larme. In the twenties his collected works were published in three volumes.

Behind Slezkin stood a new writer, just starting out, Mikhail Bulgakov. His feuilletons and *Notes on the Cuff* had been printed in the Berlin paper *On the Eve [Nakanune]*. One had to notice his unusually fresh language, exquisite dialog and unforced humor. I liked everything in *On the Eve* which came from his pen.

In one feuilleton the narrator is peacefully talking to his wife. She says: "And why are there so many crows in Moscow... they have pigeons in foreign countries... in Italy..."

"And those pigeons are real bastards too," he answers her.

A really epic phrase, like Gogol's! At once you sense that something in life is not going well for him... Before me stood a man in his early thirties, with light hair combed smooth, parted to the side. His eyes were blue, his features uneven, his nostrils cut deeply; when he talked his forehead wrinkled. But it was a face that was attractive on the whole, a face of great possibilities. I mean that it was capable of expressing the most varied feelings. I wore myself out trying to think of who Mikhail Bulgakov looked like. And suddenly it dawned on me—he looked like Chaliapin!

He was dressed in a countrified black Tolstoy shirt with no belt, like a baby's jacket. I was not used to seeing men who looked like that, and his appearance seemed rather comical to me. So did his shiny shoes with the bright yellow uppers, which I laughed at and immediately christened "chicken shoes." When we got to know each other better, he told me, not without some bitterness, "If the elegant perfumed lady had known how difficult it was for me to get those shoes, she would not have laughed."

I saw that he was touchy and easily wounded. Someone else would not have paid attention to it. At the same party he sat down at the piano and started to sing some Italian romance and to play the waltz from *Faust*... And then?

Then there was a great pause in the country. There was general confusion. Moscow was numb, confused: Lenin had died. It was more than thirty degrees below zero centigrade. There were bonfires at the cross-roads. A line of many thousands stretched out like an unbroken ribbon toward the Building of the Soviets.

A time of troubles began in my personal life. I separated from my first husband and moved in for a time with some relatives, the Tarnovskys. I met Mikhail Afanasievich in the street when the sun was already beginning to provide some warmth even though it was still freezing. He was walking along, smiling to himself at something. I told him my new address and about the changes in my life.

First among the Tarnovskys was the father, Evgeny, known as Dey at home. Later he was the model for Professor

Persikov in "The Fatal Eggs" (I will discuss that later). He was a fount of knowledge. He could quote Voltaire in the original, could recite Japanese haikus in Japanese. I was so proud when at sixteen I learned a haiku from him in the original. Dey never lectured and never forced anything on you. He simply knew a great deal, and that was sufficient to give him incontrovertible authority. Dey knew how Attila died. He could answer any question. His daughter always amazed her history teachers by contributing some special fact not in the text book, or which could never be mentioned in class about the epoch they were studying. Her name was Nadezhda Evgenievna, but in our intimate circle she was known as Gadik [literally, "little reptile"].

This was the house which welcomed Mikhail Afanasievich, hereafter referred to as M. A. He came and then started to visit almost every day. He immediately won Gadik's sympathy, especially when he started to court me.

It was already spring which was so eagerly awaited in the city. It was warm. The three of us, Gadik, M.A. and I, would sit outside under a tree. He is merry, smiling, keeping up the courtship.

"Little Gad," he says, "just think of what awaits you if there should be a favorable outcome."

"A fox coat?" she counters in the same key.

"Well, we'll just have to see about a coat. But definitely you're guaranteed boots with flaps."

"That wouldn't be enough..."

"We could add galoshes..." They both start laughing. I laugh too. But I didn't want to get married.

M. A. became friendly with Tarnovsky himself. Soon the two of them would talk animatedly about the most varied subjects and Dey fell completely under Bulgakov's spell.

"I really did a job on both the Tarnovskys," said M. A. later with a gay laugh. (When he joked he was forgiven everything. "You joke like no one else," wrote Akhmatova in her poem on Bulgakov's death.)

My stay with the Tarnovskys came to an end. Nadya's (Gadik's) husband returned from a long business trip, and they had only one room divided by a curtain. It was large, but it was still only one room.

Unfortunately the funny letter in verse written to Nadya

has not been preserved. "Oh, Gadik with the eyes of Ontario!" it began, and the contents of it warned the Tarnovskys to protect me better or "bald devils might steal Lyuba (me)."

All of our most important conversations took place near Patriarchs' Ponds (M. A. lived nearby, at 10 Sadovaya). In the course of one especially intimate conversation, during which M. A., normally the most reserved of men, was extremely frank, I was won over and gave up my inclination for the single life.

We decided to get married. That is easy to say—get married. But where was there to live? M. A. at least had a roof over his head, but I didn't even have that much. But an opportunity turned up. An old acquaintance of Gadik's came to visit her. Her name was also Nadezhda, but she was quite a bit older than we. She was small with flaming red hair, dyed. Even though she looked rather sweet, she put off many people because of her eccentricities. She was capable, for instance, of taking her breasts in her hands and exclaiming in a loud voice: "I have nice little breasts!" or talking about some love affair of hers in an unbearable boastful and immodest manner. She rather interested me. Nadya, who was much nicer and more tolerant than I, put up with her patiently; but M. A. disliked her at once and irrevocably. He christened her Mymra, [the equivalent of Dumb Dora].When he and I moved into the place on Obukhov Lane, and she took it into her head to visit us, he said: "If Mymra's coming over, I'm leaving the house." Luckily she got involved in some incredibly turbulent love affair and her visits stopped, but her portrait—caricaturized, of course—is reflected in the novella *Heart of a Dog*.

But it was this very same woman who got us temporary shelter. She lived on Arbat Lane in an ancient wooden house. I spent the nights in the room of her student brother, who'd gone off to do his on the job training.

One day when Nadezhda had gone out on business, M. A. arrived and said that we'd write a play about life in France (I had lived there for a few years), and that he already had a title: *White Clay.* I was very surprised and asked what the white clay was, what it was used for, what was made from it.

"They make china dogs from it," he answered laughing. This phrase was later spoken by one of the play's characters.

Much later, when I was reading *The Cherry Orchard*, I

ran across Simeon Pishchik's story about how some Englishmen found white clay in his garden, concluded a lease with him to develop it and gave him a cash advance. So that was where the unusual title came from! I never did manage to find out what they make from this clay besides china dogs.

But we wrote it and had a good time doing it.

The plot of the play was simple. White clay is discovered on the large and prosperous estate of the widow Duval, who lives there with her eighteen-year-old daughter. The news upsets the local landowners. No one has any idea what this stuff is. M. Paul Yves, a neighbor who is also widowed, rushes to the Duval estate to investigate and at once falls under the charm of the mistress of the house.

The mother and daughter look incredibly alike. They increase the impression by wearing almost identical clothes. They are amused by the constant misunderstandings which arise because of this. M. Yves confuses their identities and so does his son Jean, a student home from the Sorbonne on vacation, as does the Alsatian geologist, von Trupp, who has been invited to study the clay but who falls madly in love with Mme. Duval instead. M. Yves is the classical type of the jealous man. From the moment of his arrival confusion begins. He will not part with his revolver.

"That damned resemblance!" he cries. "I want to shoot the mother but I end up aiming at the daughter..."

There are confessions of love, a chase, a fight, and suicide threats. When they finally manage to trick the jealous man into giving up the revolver it turns out to be unloaded. In the third act all ends happily. Here we utilized the principle of the tongue twister—Yakh married Tsip, Yakhtsidrakh married Tsiptsidrip, and so on. Paul Yves marries the mother, his son the daugher, and Von Trupp marries M. Yves' housekeeper, Mme. Melanie.

Our dream was to see *White Clay* at the Korsh Theater with Radin as M. Yves and Toporkov as von Trupp.

We showed two finished acts to Alexander Nikolaevich Tikhonov (Serebrov), a Moscow editor. He said with typical gruff bluntness, "Come on, think a bit, who wants a society comedy now?"

So we never completed the third act. There is not one

trace of this play in the Lenin Library archive unfortunately.

My life in the student's room ended. Nadezhda's brother returned from his job training...

We went to register our marriage at a repulsive office of the Bureau of Registration of Civil Status in Glazovsky Lane (now Lunacharsky Street), overlooking the Church of the Saviour of the Sepulchre.

M. A.'s sister, Nadezhda Afanasievna Zemskaya took us to the bosom of her family. She was a school principal and lived on the second floor of a building which had been a tsarist gymnasium (high school). The result was like the old woman in the shoe. In it lived: she, her husband Andrei Mikhailovich Zemsky, their little daughter Olga, Andrei's sister Katya, Nadezhda's sister Vera. So there were five people already, and they were expecting the arrival of Nadezhda's younger sister Elena Bulgakova from Kiev. Then we turned up too.

Luckily it was summer, so they put us up in the staff room, on an oilcloth sofa, which I used to slip off of during the night. It stood beneath a portrait of a stern Ushinsky. There were other portraits too, but none so stern and therefore memorable.

Nadezhda Afanasievna took in all her relatives with an amazing gentleness and enviable patience, as if it could be no other way. She had a highly developed desire to unify and consolidate the Bulgakov family, rather than scatter it.

I never saw so many philologists at one time in a private home as I saw there. Nadezhda herself, her husband and her sister Elena were philologists, as were three constant visitors to the house, one of whom, Mikhail Vasilievich Svetlaev, soon became Elena's husband.

Nature had painted the Bulgakovs in pale colors. They all had blue eyes and were fair, after their mother, with the exception of the youngest, Elena. She had gray eyes and luxuriant dark brown hair. There was something childish in her face, it was so round that it could have been drawn with a compass.

Nadezhda was the sister who was closest to M. A. There was a spiritual bond between them, and it was easier for him to communicate with her than with anyone else. But his sister Elena could also be a worthy partner in jokes. I remember that I gave the Zemsky family a lampshade I'd made myself from some flowery material. Elena labeled my present a "union of town and country," which better than anything conveyed the spirit of the times.

Nadezhda Afanasievna's husband, Andrei Mikhailovich was very tolerant of the way in which his family was expanding. He was a reserved and tactful man.

One day M. A. and I ran into one of his colleagues from the newspaper *The Whistle (Gudok)*, the journalist Aaron Erlich. The men stopped to talk for a minute on the street. I stood to one side and noticed that Erlich was glancing at me while he talked. When M. A. returned I asked what Aaron had said.

"He just said stupid things," he answered, half-smiling, half-embarrassed. But I insisted so he confessed that he'd said: "Even a monkey would look pretty if it's dressed in white." (I was wearing a white suit). M. A. and I made jokes about the monkey for a long time after that...

Many years later Aaron Erlich published a book, *Life Taught Us (Nas uchil zhizn')*. Published in Moscow in 1960, it has quite a few pages devoted to Bulgakov. But it would have been better if these pages had not been written at all. The author constantly fences himself off from the memory of his former colleague and comrade, worrying that somebody might suddenly get the idea that he, Erlich, was ever friendly with that "bad boy." Therefore he is quick to tell whatever may be unflattering to Bulgakov, condemning even his manner of joking. "Sometimes he made you prick up your ears by the very tendency of his jokes." Of course this is not very grammatical, but the idea is obvious.

However nicely we lived under Ushinsky's wings, we still needed our own roof. I remembered a building on Karetnaya-Sadovaya from many years before, where my oldest sister's wedding had been held. It was a beautiful building with columns, facing a shady garden where the hostess' son and I played hide and seek. I was nine years old and he was eleven. I was the youngest one at that wedding, but they gave me some champagne anyway, which made me very happy; the whole time I was afraid they'd notice and try to take it away from me. I don't know which impressed me more, the hostess Varvara Vasilievna (my sister's godmother), so pretty in her dark green dress which matched her eyes, or that champagne.

Now, in 1924, I decided to go to her and ask if she could help us in our search for refuge. I recognized the building at once, but the plaque of some institute hung on it. Varvara Vasilievna herself lived in the courtyard in a wooden addition. Instead of the former beauty, an old woman with a black nun-like wimple on her head met me, a Lady of Our Sorrows—she had buried both her sons. She was very friendly, and was glad to take me across to some out of the way corner to one of the shacks where they did repairs. I was supposed to come back the next day to talk it over, but I never went. It was true that what we took instead turned out to be no better, but at least the area was respectable. At that time we were introduced to a man who was very, very sad. His eyes were so mournful that I can still remember them. He it was who took us to the apartment where we finally settled: 9, Obukhov Lane.

Photo of Lyubov Bulgakova.

IN THE DOVECOTE

We are living in the ramshackle little addition in the courtyard of No. 9 Obukhov Lane, now Chisty Lane. On the building next door, No. 7, a commemorative plaque is displayed: "The outstanding composer Sergei Ivanovich Taneev, and the eminent scholar and statesman Vladimir Ivanovich Taneev lived and worked in this building." What unsightly homes these famous people chose for themselves!

We name our house the "Dovecote." This is our first home together. The dovecote was a lucky place: the play *The Days of the Turbins*, "The Fatal Eggs," and *Heart of a Dog* (the last dedicated to me) were all written here. But all of this comes later, and in the meantime M. A. is working as a columnist for *The Whistle*. He takes my little suitcase (nick-named "puppy" —we are fond of nicknames) and goes to the editorial office. He brings home letters from readers, individuals or groups of workers, the letters are brought home in the puppy. At night we read them aloud to each other, and select the most interesting ones for the column. I remember several of the funny episodes. In my memory there is the clear image of one Ferapont Bubenchikov, picked up somewhere in the newspaper world, or more likely thought up by Bulgakov himself. He was a boastful, pushy fellow, and M. A. spoke of him in the third person, with a sly smile: "You know Ferapont Bubenchikov," or " 'We don't care,' said Ferapont," or "That's not Ferapont Bubenchikov."

Many years later I came upon issue No. 15, 1926, of the humorous magazine *The Laugher (Smekhach)*. In it was something titled "The Golden Correspondence of Ferapont Ferapontovich Kaportsev." So Ferapont remained persistently in the head of Bulgakov the journalist. But it is no wonder: in the twenties he'd gotten interested in a remarkable little book, *Venediktov, or Memorable Events of my Life*. The book lover Ferapont appears in the work, and obviously Bulgakov then became very fond of the name.

But I will tell about that book further on.

An entire Pleiade of writers came out of *The Whistle* (how lucky for that magazine!): Mikhail Bulgakov, Yury Olesha —then still only a columnist known as "Zubilo" who wrote in verse on topics of the day, and Valentin Kataev and later his brother Evgeny Petrov, all of them worked there. Olesha remembers those days touchingly in his memoirs.

Later at some festivity at the paper, Olesha read the epigram he'd dedicated to Bulgakov:

> Treating everyone the same
> Clinking his rusty pen
> Was Bulgakov the rewrite man,
> But today he's the evil of the day.

Mikhail Afanasievich wrote quickly, almost in bursts. This is what he himself has to say about the matter: "It took me between eighteen and twenty minutes, including time out for smoking and whistling, to write a column of 75 lines. To have it typed, including giggling with the typist, took eight minutes. In a word, a half an hour and it was all finished."

I recently re-read more than a hundred of Bulgakov's feuilletons printed in *The Whistle*. He signed them differently, but in spite of the various pseudonyms it is still possible to recognize his "handwriting." No matter how light Bulgakov himself made of his work as a rewriter, it played a certain role in his creative work by serving as a springboard for his moving to serious literary work. His grasp of plot, his easy dialog, his inventiveness and humor—it is all here.

I have mentioned that we enjoyed nicknames. M. A. happened to remember once the child's verse which tells of a mean, clever orangutang with three sons, Mika, Maka, and Mikukha. And, he added: I am Maka. The most surprising thing was that this self-assigned nickname stuck very quickly. Soon none of his friends called him anything else, and his closest friend, Kolya Lyamin said affectionately, "Makin." M. A. himself often signed things Mak or Maka. I will sometimes call him that here.

We live on the second floor. The entire upper floor is divided into three apartments, two along the front, one on the side. In the middle there is a corridor, and in the corner of the corridor there is a stove. We cook on it and it heats our room. In one ugly little room there lives Anna Alexandrovna, an elderly, once beautiful woman. She had married into a titled family and her maiden name was an ancient one, celebrated by Pushkin. She was a widow, completely lost and helpless, and suffering from asthma as well. She lived with her young daughter; kind people had taken the two boys. Marya Vlasievna, a simple woman lives in the other little cubicle. She sells coffee and pies on Sukharevka. The two women hate each other fiercely. We are the buffer zone between two warring states. In the morning when Marya Vlasievna is arranging a complicated metal construction around her neck (so the coffee and pies won't get cold) you can hear from Anna Alexandrova's cubicle, with a certain tragic intonation:

"My silver spoon is missing again!"

"If you put things where they belong nothing would be missing," says Marya Vlasievna in her low voice already on the way out.

We keep quiet. I feel sorry for Anna, but I like Marya better. She is more intelligent and more cordial. I like the fact that she does everything well. Sometimes her daughter who lives nearby leaves her four-year-old son Vitka with her. The grandmother worships this rather repulsive little boy. M.A. loves children and knows how to get along with them, especially boys. It is apropos to mention the story "A Psalm," about a mother and child, which has been dated wrongly 1926. But it is from 1923 (published in *On the Eve)*. By 1926 Bulgakov was no longer writing in that style.

When Vitka's crying bothered us too much, we took him into our room and let him sit on the foot stool. At this point I usually shirked my duty, and Vitka passed entirely into M.A.'s hands. M.A. showed him tricks. I can still hear his voice saying: "Here is a box on the table. It's in front of you. One, two, three! Now where is the box?"

I remember the beginning of a Bulgakov sketch written from nature:

Evening. The faucet: drip... drip... drip...

Vitka (whining): Marya Vlasievna...

M.V. Coming, coming little man. I'm coming right now, Jesus Christ...

Her daughter Tatyana was a real Russian beauty. She was statuesque, and had light brown hair and dark blue eyes. She could have been the heroine of a Koltsov poem, or a Georgian song. M.A. says that she is nice to look at.

Downstairs in the front room lives a man with a black beard and an invisible family. Around the holidays all of them sing country songs merrily. When we would come home we'd see a shiny brass samovar with ring-shaped buns hanging from it, shining through the window.

A young policeman lives below us. Now and then he beats his wife—"teaches her," as Marya puts it—and then she lies down in the entrance hall and cries. I wanted to interfere, to go out to her and comfort her, but M.A. said: "You're going to get into trouble Lyubasha. No good deed will go unpunished." Then a sly glance from the blue eyes in my direction and the addition: "That's what the English say."

All the residents of the Dovecote have their own guests: Marya has Tatyana and Vitka, and sometimes the son-in-law, a devil-may-care barber, who lives in a state of semi-drunkenness. Frequently an old, decrepit eighty-year-old woman comes to stand under Anna's window. It seems that if a wind were to blow, the formerly titled and beautiful countess would fly away. She wears a wide-brimmed hat (perhaps the brim keeps her on the ground). In the spring a bunch of violets adorns her hat, in the winter a piece of ermine is draped over the brim. The old woman speaks softly, looking in the window of the Dovecote: "L'Impératrice vous salut," and then loudly in Russian: "The Empress greets you." Curious heads pop out from the bottom windows. What was she dreaming of, the old maid of honor, what does she think about while her daughter runs around from morning until night giving French lessons?

"Calm down the old woman," M.A. said to me. "I'm thinking of her own good..."

Our own frequent guests were Nikolai Lyamin and his wife, the artist Natalia Ushakova. During my eight years of marriage to M.A. these two remained our closest friends. I will have reason to bring them up often.

The surgeon Nikolai Glodyrevsky, an old crony of M.A.'s from Kiev, and friend of their family, used to come to see us often. He worked in Professor Martynov's clinic, and would stop by our place on the way home. M.A. always enjoyed talking to him. M.A. asked him for some surgical details when he was describing the operation in *Heart of a Dog*. But it was Glodyrevsky who took Maka to Professor Martynov, and the latter made him enter the clinic—for an appendix operation. All of this was decided very suddenly, unexpectedly.

We were allowed to see M.A. right after the operation. He was so pitiful, just like a bedraggled chicken. I brought food to him, but he was irritable the whole time because he was hungry— his diet was restricted. This wasn't like it is nowadays when you get meat almost the day after an operation. A children's book by Sofia Fedorchenko came out about that time, and her description of the tiger exactly fit my Maka: "Always hungry and angry at the world."

Later that winter Glodyrevsky took us to Professor Martynov's for a musical soirée. I have forgotten whether it was a quartet or a trio, but it was made up only of doctors.

I don't know what sort of doctor M. A. was, "sawbones with honors," as he styles himself in his autobiographical sketch, but the medical profession, not to mention its deeper influence, helped him a great deal when he had to write things concerning medicine, such as the chapters in "The Fatal Eggs" about the experiments. The story's Professor Persikov works in a lab and knows how to deal with a microscope because the author himself in real life knew those things. And likewise in the operation of *Heart of a Dog*, the author is familiar with the details of operations. The reader always appreciates and senses that the author is well informed.

M. A. dedicated his rapidly written fantastic tale "The Fatal Eggs," (October, 1924), the novella *Heart of a Dog* (1925), and the play *Adam and Eve* (1931) to the problem of man's creative genius, to the power of knowledge and the triumph of intellect.

Persikov, in "The Fatal Eggs," discovers a previously unknown ray which stimulates reproduction and growth, imparting extraordianry vital energy to living organisms. It is not Persikov's fault that a catastrophe takes place due to the mistakes made by ignorant people and bureaucrats; the consequence is the death of countless victims and the destruction of both the inventor and invention.

When he described Professor Persikov's appearance and some of his habits, M. A. used as his model the figure of a living person, my relative Evgeny Nikitich Tarnovsky,whom I described in Chapter One. He was also a professor like Persikov, but of a subject far removed from zoology; he was a specialist in criminal statistics. As for his general erudition, it was extraordinary and it was bound to impress a person like M.A., who took everything in so greedily, and who was so creatively inquisitive.

The scientist in the novella *Heart of a Dog*, Professor of Surgery, Philip Philippovich Preobrazhensky, is based on M. A.'s uncle, Nikolai Mikhailovich Pokrovsky. He was the brother of M. A.'s mother, Varvara Mikhailovna, who is so touchingly called "Bright Queen" in *White Guard*.

Nikolai Mikhailovich Pokrovsky was a doctor specializing in gynecology, and he had been the assistant to the well-known Professor Snegirev. He lived on the corner of Prechistenka and Obukhov Lane, a few houses away from our Dovecote. His brother, dear Mikhail Mikhailovich, who specialized in internal medicine was a bachelor and lived there too. In addition, two nieces also found shelter in the same apartment. One of M. A.'s brothers, Nikolai, was also a doctor.

I would like to make a digression on the subject of the younger brother Nikolai. The noble, appealing personality of Nikolai Turbin was always dear to my heart (especially as it is shown in the novel *White Guard*—in the play, *Days of the Turbins* he is much more sketchily drawn). In real life I never had the opportunity to meet Nikolai Afanasievich Bulgakov. This younger representative of the Bulgakov family's favorite profession was a doctor of medicine, a bacteriologist, a scientist and researcher. He died in Paris in 1966.

He studied at the University of Zagreb, and then worked there in the Department of Bacteriology. He and the Croat doctor, Sertich, collaborated on several scientific works which caught the attention of the Parisian scientist, Professor Felix d'Herelle, who discovered the bacteriophage in 1917. After organizing his own institute in Paris for the study and production of bacteriophages for medical use, d'Herelle invited the young scientists from Zagreb to join him.

N. A. Bulgakov was involved not just in the bacteriophages themselves, but also in designing and inventing all sorts of scientific apparatus.

In one of his books, Professor d'Herelle relates how he sent a streptococcus culture to Paris from London with instructions to find the bacteriophage which would destroy it. After only two weeks his desire had been accomplished. "To do that kind of work," wrote d'Herelle, "it had to be Bulgakov, with his abilities and precise methods."

In 1936 d'Herelle sent Nikolai Afanasievich to Mexico in his place, to organize the teaching of bacteriology there. This task was accomplished, and Bulgakov organized a bacteriological laboratory there. He was lecturing in Spanish within six months. During the German occupation of France Nikolai Afanasievich, being a Yugoslav citizen, was sent to a camp near Compiegne as a hostage. He worked as a doctor there, and demonstrated what an unusually good man he was, dealing with every misfortune. This is what those who knew him well say.

At the end of the war a special American commission, interested in transporting bacteriophages to the USA, arrived in Paris to inspect the laboratory. N. A. Bulgakov showed the Americans not only his extensive collection of live microbes, but also the functioning of the machine that filled and sealed the capsules of the bacteriophages under sterile conditions. The question of transport to the USA was solved satisfactorily...

Sometimes I imagine to myself the happy meeting the two brothers would have had. They are there, walking along the banks of the Seine, the older one and the younger, and they talk, talk endlessly. It was always M. A.'s cherished dream to visit Paris—he was both an admirer of and expert on Molière. It is revealing that he wrote in the first edition of his novel *The Days of the Turbins* (the Paris publishing house Concorde published *White Guard* under this title in 1927): "This copy is given to my dear wife Lyuba, printed in my unattainable city. July 3, 1929." In that same year M. A. wrote a touching inscription to me in a copy of the *Diaboliad* collection: "To my friend, that good fellow Lyubochka, and to Muka too. M. Bulgakov, March 27, 1928. Moscow." Muka was the cat, and its name will come up again.

But let us return to Phillip Philippovich Preobrazhensky, or rather, Nikolai Mikhailovich Pokrovsky, as he was named in real life. He was renowned for his violent temper and intractable character which caused one of his nieces to remark: "There is no pleasing Uncle Kolya; he says: Don't you dare have a baby, but don't you dare have an abortion either." Both of the Pokrovsky brothers treated their numerous female relatives.

On St. Nicholas' Day [December 6] everyone gathered around the name-day dinner table, where, as M.A. put it, the name-day celebrator, Nikolai Mikhailovich, was enthroned "like some Lord of Sabaoth." His wife, Maria Silovna, put pies on the table. A silver coin was baked into one of them. Whoever found it was considered lucky, and his health would be drunk. The Lord of Sabaoth loved to tell simple jokes and then distort them so that they were unrecognizable, which made the merry young company laugh.

Nikolai Mikhailovich Pokrovsky never discovered that he was the prototype for the great surgeon Preobrazhensky who changed a dog into a man by operating on his brain. But the scientist in the novella made a mistake: he did not study the laws of heredity . By implanting the pituitary gland of the dead man he imparted to the dog all the vices of the deceased: the inclination to lie and steal, coarseness, alcoholism and the potential for murder. The good dog turns into a worthless man. The operation scene cannot be read without agitation.

The third genuis-like inventor is the professor of chemistry, the Academician Efrosimov, of the fantastic play *Adam and Eve* (1931). I will discuss this work at greater length later on.

Since he had published the story "The Fatal Eggs" the chief editor of the Nedra Publishing house, Nikolai Semenovich Angarsky (Klestov) also wanted to publish *Heart of a Dog*. I don't know which channels, besides the ones inside the publishing house, this work had to pass through, but time went on and nothing happened. One time Angarsky came over to the Dovecote and told us that he was working hard in high places to get it published, but it hadn't worked out yet. We very much appreciated these words of assurance from him; we could discern sincere interest in what he said.

But to tell the truth, I was a little afraid of this tall man with the red mephisthophelean beard: a lot was already said about his intolerance and sharp personality. One time, laughing, M. A. told a story about Angarsky:

> An author brought a manuscript to the editorial office. N. S. said to him when he was still some distance away: "The heroine's Nina? Forget it!"

But once after a party for the editorial workers, (I remember Boris Leontevich Leontev, Natalia Pavlovna Vitman and the nice secretary in Peter Nikolaevich Zaitsev's office). I had the opportunity to talk with Angarsky about literature, and I saw from the little he said that he knew and understood it with a *real* love, not an opportunistic one. From that evening on I ceased to be afraid of him and to this day I remember with gratitude his liking for M.A. which can also be explained by that very love for Russian literature.

One time Angarsky, his wife, a very pleasant woman, (and a doctor), arrived along with their three children in a large open car. They came to take us out for a drive out into the forest to pick mushrooms. We got to the forest, near Zvenigorod. The children ran into the forest and returned with slippery jacks. Angarsky said "those are not mushrooms," and kept on disappointing the children, who had long faces due to this. M.A. and I glanced stealthily at each other and both of us remembered the "heroine Nina," and many times afterwards we recalled Nikolai Semenovich's brusque temper which could certainly be seen in other things besides mushroom matters. He perished, I heard, during the terrible Stalin years.

At about that time we made the acquaintance of the writer Vikenty Veresaev. He was also very favorably disposed toward Bulgakov. Even though their works tended to go in completely opposite directions, their similar experiences when they first started to practice medicine were bound to bring them together. One only needs to read Veresaev's *Notes of a Doctor* and Bulgakov's *Notes of a Young Doctor*.

We went to the Veresaevs' many times. I remember clearly his wife Maria who had a particularly radiant smile. I remember their long table. Among the guests one noticed especially the handsome gray head and contrasting black brows of the well-known Pushkin scholar Professor Mstislav Tsyavlovsky, and at his side, inseparable, sits his very feminine wife, Tatyana Zenger, also a Pushkin scholar. I remember that apropos of Pushkin's opponent Vikenty Vikentievich said: "Just by looking at d'Anthes' portrait, it is immediately clear that it is the picture of a real degenerate."

I was about to open my mouth and say aloud, for the sake of justice that d'Anthes was very handsome, but I caught M.A. giving me a stern look and I bit my tongue.

I liked Veresaev. There was something substantial in the whole appearance of the old doctor and revolutionary. And if a black cat ran between the two of them later, as people said, it can only be regretted.

I will digress now. I have in front of me the magazine *Literary Questions (Voprosy literatury)*, v. II, 1965, in which the correspondence between Bulgakov and Veresaev is published concerning their work on the play *Pushkin (Last Days)*, a correspondence which sheds light on the "black cat." At first it was understood that the Pushkin expert Veresaev would be the source of information, a consultant. Bulgakov would be the playwright, that is, the person who converts this information into dramatic form. What really happened? At first all seemed to go well, but then Bulgakov's unique and unusual approach to Pushkin as a dramatic character gradually begins to irritate Veresaev, and as a writer he starts to feel that the limited role of consultant is too narrow for him. He cannot help but intrude upon the area of the dramatist, and does it rather brusquely at times. But he runs into opposition. The character of d'Anthes was the special bone of contention.

The tone of both of their letters is one of restrained irritation, and I think both of them had a bitter aftertaste afterwards. In the end M. A. "fought off" Vikenty Vikentievich's attacks; his talent as a dramatist and his knowledge and feeling for staging gave him the advantage in the polemic.

The last short letter is dated March 12, 1939, one year before M. A.'s death. I do not know if Veresaev ever saw *Pushkin* on the stage, but Bulgakov did not live to see the opening night.

I will now return to the interrupted story. Time went by, and clouds began to gather above the novella *Heart of a Dog*, clouds we did not suspect existed.

"One fine evening"—that is how all stories begin—one unfine evening someone knocked at the door of our Dovecote. (We had no bell.) To my question "Who is it?" came the brisk voice of our landlord: "It's me, bringing you some guests."

Two men in civilian clothes stood on the threshold: one with a pince-nez, and one who was just short—Investigator Slavkin and his assistant, with a search warrant. The landlord was along as a witness. Bulgakov wasn't home and I got worried: how was he going to react to the arrival of these "guests"?

So I asked them not to start the search without the master of the house being present, and said that he would be arriving shortly.

Everybody came into the room and sat down. The landlord lounged in the armchair in the middle. He had a very strong personality, and unrestrained language, especially after a glass or two... Silence. But unfortunately it didn't last long.

"Have you heard the joke." began the landlord...

(Lord, let this pass, I thought.)

"This Jew is standing on Lubianka Square and a passer-by asks him: 'Do you know where the National Insurance [*Gosstrakh*, as abbreviated in Russian, with *strakh* meaning fear by itself] is?'

'I don't know about the National Insurance, but the National Horror [*gosuzhas*, a reference to the Lubianka Prison] is right here.'"

The joke teller shakes with laughter. I manage a feeble smile. Slavkin and his assistant remain silent. The silence continues—then suddenly a familiar knock.

I rushed to the door and whispered to M. A.:

"Don't get upset, Maka, they're doing a search."

But he remained perfectly cool then (he began to twitch much later). Slavkin worked on the book shelves. The "pince-nez" began turning over the arm chairs and poking them with long needles.

And then the unexpected occurred. M. A. said:

"Well, Lyuba, if they shoot up your chairs I'm not going to be held responsible." (I'd bought these old chairs at a warehouse for confiscated furniture, for three rubles fifty apiece.)

Laughter overcame us. Perhaps it was nervous.

Near morning the yawning landlord asked:

"Why can't you comrades transfer your activities to the daytime hours?"

No one answered him. As soon as they found *Heart of a Dog* and the diaries on the shelf the "guests" left.

Heart of a Dog was only returned two years later, at Gorky's insistence...

Once two men came to the Dovecote. They were both tall, but very different. One was younger than we, the other was much older. The young dark man had dark dreamy eyes, sharp features and a haughty expression. He stooped, in the posture usual for those with weak chests, inclined to tuberculosis. It was difficult to guess his nationality: Georgian, Jewish, Romanian, perhaps Hungarian? The other man was dressed in the usual uniform of those days, a peasant shirt, and looked like a smart engineer.

They turned out to be from the Vakhtangov Theater. The younger one was the actor Vasily Vasilievich Kuza (he died during the bombing, in the first days of the war); the older one was the director Alexei Dmitrievich Popov. They wanted M. A. to write a comedy for the theater.

Later when he was looking through the local news in the evening paper *The Red Gazette* (there existed such a paper then), M. A. happened to see an announcement that the police had discovered a gambling den, operating under the cover of a sewing shop, in the apartment of a certain Zoya Buyalskaya. This is how the basic idea for the play *Zoya's Apartment* came about. Everything else about the play—the plot, the characters, the situations—comes out of the author's imagination, and demonstrates brilliantly the talent and innate feeling for the stage the author had. Popov directed the play, and the premiere was October 28, 1926.

S. P. Isakov, who died recently, did the scenery. And I must do justice to the actors, who played with great verve. It was fascinating of course to play negative characters in the context of all the positive characters that were overcrowding the Soviet stage of those days, and vice, as we all know, has more scenic colors than virtue. All the characters here were negative. One can truthfully state that there are no "true blue roles" in this play. It enjoyed great success and ran for over two years. Cross my heart, I can't understand what is criminal about the play, and why it was banned.

In addition to the high quality of the actors' performances I remember the unusually well done city noise which came into the apartment through the wide open window, and along with this I recall a minor but rather funny touch.

In several of the first public rehearsals Mansurova played Zoya almost without makeup, but then the director Popov demanded that she change her appearance. A nose was glued onto her, and this annoyed the actress a great deal. This may seem funny, but it was precisely the nose that in some way intensified the comic aspects of the character. Obviously this was the result the director wanted to achieve.

"When I think now of how the production was subjected to such harsh criticism." writes the director and actress of the Art Theater M. Knebel in her book *My Whole Life* (Moscow, 1967), "then I am convinced that one of the reasons for it was the genre itself—or rather the fact that it was such an unusual genre." This is one of her arguments, and there is another: "The Vakhtangov actress A.A. Orochko changed the negative character Alla to one that sounded positive through her interpretation. And she did this so convincingly that she supposedly contributed to the taking off of the play." This is not true of course. Neither I, for instance, nor any of my friends remember Orochko at all in this role. Later on Popov repudiated his production of *Zoya's Apartment*. "The director's repudiation was a tribute to the times," says Knebel. She does not say it all, however. The real tribute to the times was the ostracism, not yet total, to which Bulgakov's works were being subjected.

Ostankino Park, 1926. Left to right: S. S. Topleninov, L. E. Bulgakova, M. A. Bulgakov, N. N. Lyamin.

A READING AT THE LYAMINS'

M. A. made the acquaintance of Nikolai Nikolaevich Lyamin in 1925 and a long friendship followed. There is a copy of the collection *Diaboliad* (Nedra, 1925) with a touching dedication: "To my very best friend Nikolai Nikolaevich Lyamin. Mikhail Bulgakov, Moscow, July 18, 1925." They first met at the home of the painter Sergei Sergeevich Zayaitsky where Bulgakov had read excerpts from *White Guard*. Since then he had read virtually all of his writings at the Lyamins' (Nikolai Nikolaevich and his wife, the artist Natalia Abramovna Ushakova): *White Guard* (in excerpts), "The Fatal Eggs," *Heart of a Dog, Zoya's Apartment, The Crimson Island, Molière*, and "The Consultant With a Hoof" which was the basis for the novel *The Master and Margarita*.

He told me before the first reading that "highly qualified" persons would be listening to him (I had not yet been to their house). Such an expression, not at all typical of M. A., made me look at the listeners with special attention.

I remembered the sharp-witted and cheerful Sergei Sergeevich Zayaitsky; the handsome Mikhail Mikhailovich Morozov who had timid eyes and was a well-known Shakespeare scholar; the blustering Fyodor Alexandrovich Petrovsky, a classical philologist who taught Latin literature at the Moscow University; Sergei Vasilievich Shervinsky, poet and translator; and the theater director and translator Vladimir Emilievich Morits and his charming wife Alexandra Sergeevna. Frequent visitors also were the art critics Andrei Alexandrovich Guber, and Boris Valentinovich Shaposhnikov; Alexander Georgievich Gabrichevsky, later a corresponding member of the Academy of Architecture; the writer Vladimir Nikolaevich Vladimirov (Dolgoruky), a translator and our "court" poet; Nikolai Nikolaevich Volkov, a philosopher and artist; and Vsevolod Mikhailovich Avilov, the son of the writer Lidia Avilova (about whom I.S. Bunin wrote so rapturously in his memoirs). At the request of the listeners V. M. Avilov invariably read children's poems about a little frog.

I also remember the homely, typically Russian, even simple but infinitely sweet face of Anna Ilinichna Tolstoy. One writer used the following cliche in describing her in his *Literary Memoirs* (and he only saw her once): "Since she was Tolstoy's granddaughter she must have a high forehead; being a countess meant she had small aristocratic hands. Actually it was the reverse: low forehead and large hands, a masculine but handsome figure." M. A. spoke of her appearance as "the very image of her grandfather, only the beard is missing." Sometimes Anna Ilinichna brought her guitar. I have heard many different singers perform romances and old songs, but no one sang as our dear Anna did. Nowadays I always turn off the radio when they play for instance "The Garden Gate" in a contemporary rendition. It makes me feel ill at ease. A. I. sang in a very simple manner but her voice seemed to caress the words. The result was especially sincere somehow. But no wonder. They loved to sing at the Tolstoy home. Anna Ilinichna lived at Yasnaya Polyana until she was sixteen years old. Lev Nikolaevich also loved to hear her sing. He became especially fond of the song "The Spring Comes, Beckons, Calls." I was told this by Anna Ilinichna with whom I became very friendly. Beside her is her husband, the logician, philosopher and literary critic Pavel Sergeevich Popov, who later became friends with M. A. Sometimes she was accompanied on guitar by Nikolai Petrovich Sheremetev (a nice person), sometimes by the artist Sergei Sergeevich Topleninov, but more often she herself ran her fingers over the strings. When she was little people asked her: "What do you want to be when you grow up?" and she replied: "A horse or a singer."

Ivan Mikhailovich Moskvin sang in an equally simple manner, but A. I. sounded better just the same. I remember when Mikhail Afanasievich for the first time brought me to meet Anna Ilinichna Tolstoy and her husband Pavel Sergeevich Popov. They were living at 10, Plotnikov Lane near the Arbat in a small basement apartment, subsequently immortalized in the novel *The Master and Margarita*. I really do not know what it was about the basement that caught Bulgakov's fancy. It is true that the room with two windows was more attractive than the other one, as narrow as an intestine...

In the hallway the boxer puppy Grigory Poatapych was lying with his paws stretched out. He was drunk.

"I put a wineglass in the hallway; it's colder there," said the hostess... "And he lapped at it."

In the dining room sat a handsome young man who smiled goodnaturedly. It was a friend of the family, Petya Turkestanov. This particular evening the Lyamins were there too. I did not then have any presentiment that I would become friends with Anna Ilinichna Tolstoy for many years and with what grief I would endure her death...

I remember the writer Natalia Alexseevna Venkstern, who smoked much and greedily, and N. N. Lyamin's childhood friend the well-known Shapespeare expert M.M. Morozov, who was good-looking in a strange and disturbing sort of way.

Actors also used to come to the Lyamins': Ivan Mikhailovich Moskvin, Viktor Yakovlevich Stanitsyn, Mikhail Mikhailovich Yanshin, Cecilia Lvovna Mansurova and Elena Dmitrievna Ponsova.

Everybody listened carefully. They grasped the humor immediately. M. A. read brilliantly; expressively but without theatrical affectations. He led his listeners up to the funny parts with a light touch, almost seriously, only his eyes were laughing...

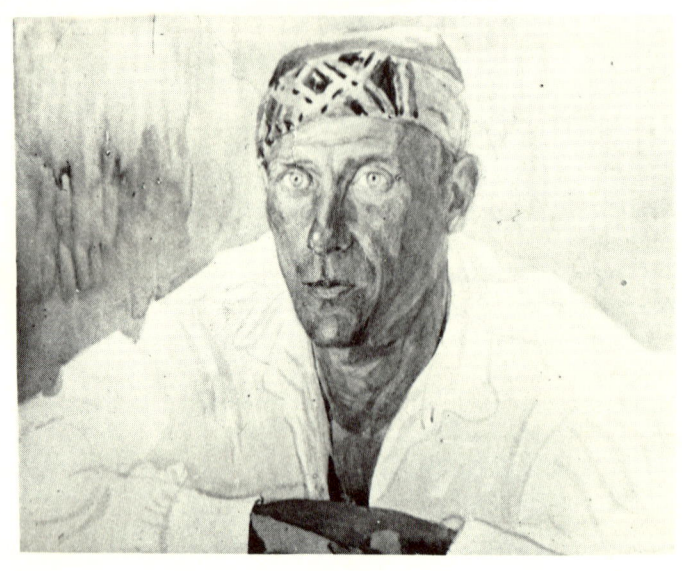

Koktebel, 1925. Drawing of Bulgakov by Anna Ostroumova-Lebedeva.

KOKTEBEL – THE CRIMEA

Summer came, but we did not know where we should go. The word Koktebel [now known as Planerskoe—trans.] was currently in the air; many people mentioned the fact that the poet Maximilian Voloshin was giving over his whole property at Koktebel for the use of writers completely free of charge. We bought Dr. Sarkisov-Serazin's guide to the Crimea. Of Koktebel he wrote that nature there was extremely poor and cheerless. There was nowhere to go for walks. People had to go many kilometers away even to pick flowers. Staying at Koktebel is made even more unpleasant by the fact that constant winds blow there. They have a depressing effect on the psyche, and persons with unstable nervous systems come back from Koktebel with their nerves even more shattered than before. I'm quoting from memory, but pretty correctly.

M. A. and I laughed at Dr. Sarkisov-Serazin's impartiality and we decided to go to Voloshin's anyway, in spite of our friend Kolya Lyamin's parting words. He said, "Well, where are you going? The Crimea is pure vulgarity. Only the cypresses are worth anything."

In verse it sounded like this:

> *My door is open. Step over the threshold*
> *My house is open in all directions.*
> (M. Voloshin, "The Poet's House," 1926)

In prose, however, it sounded more prosaic and businesslike: "There are no servants. We carry our own water. Definitely not a resort. Free and friendly communal living where anyone suitable becomes a full-fledged member. For all of this to happen it is necessary to have a cheerful attitude toward life, a love for people, and a contribution to make to our intellectual life." (From a personal letter from M. Voloshin, May 24, 1924).

And now on towards Feodosia, the final goal!

The village was far away from the sea. The poet Voloshin's house was on the edge of the shore itself.

Since my childhood the image of Pushkin's young poet Lensky had been preserved in one of my brain cells. "Always speaking with fervor and with his black curls down to his shoulders." And here before us stood a strong man with a paunch, wearing a long belted shirt and knee-length trousers, with broad shoulders, a wide face, and muscular legs in sandals. He had a bearded face with a broad forehead and broad nose. His gray-streaked light brown hair was bound with a leather strap around the forehead, and he looked like a friendly lion with his small intelligent eyes. It seemed that he ought to speak with a strong and loud bass voice, but he spoke softly and with an extremely intelligent tone of voice. He read poetry the same way—in a relaxed and unrestrained way—although I.A. Bunin says in his memoirs, and not very benevolently, I might add, that when Voloshin recited his poetry "he acted like an Olympian God, the Thunderer and would start to howl loudly and languidly... After he had finished he immediately threw off this threatening and pompous mask." (Bunin, *Complete Works*, v.9, p. 425). I will mention in passing that we never noticed Maximilian Alexandrovich doing anything calculated for effect during the month that we could observe him every day. On the contrary, he appeared to be natural and harmonious in spite of his extravagant appearance.

Some distance away in the shadow of this monumental figure stood a small woman with a skull-cap on her short hair — women with short hair were rare in those days. Everything about her made her look like a turn of the century student at the Bestuzhev Institute. She gave us a friendly smile. This was Maria Stepanovna, Maximilian Voloshin's wife.

Behind the major building, the poet's house, there is a two-story house in the distance, and closer is something like a Tartar hut, a house with no foundation, which has been sheltering the newlyweds Leonid Leonov and his wife. She is as thin as a reed, and lisps sweetly and says "sherry tree" for "cherry tree," and even Leonid Maximovich is not especially good at sibilants. M. A. and I liked it and we sometimes talked like that to each other when we were alone.

They put us up on the bottom floor of the distant two story house. Our neighbor was the poet Georgy Arkadievich Shengeli. Later on a female neighbor appeared as well, his wife who was also a poetess, Nina Leontievna, if my memory does not fail me. She was a very nice and feminine person.

The artist Anna Ostroumova-Lebedeva arrived with her husband Sergei Lebedev, whose name was subsequently immortalized as that of the chemical scientist who created synthetic rubber. They were an unusually nice couple. She was small and not very pretty but charming, and he was tall and handsome. With their behavior and manner they affirmed the truth that the more substantial is a person's inner equipment, the kinder, more outgoing, more sympathetic he is in his relations with others. During my whole life this truth has not deceived me a single time.

To tell the truth, we did not like Koktebel. We looked around; not only were there no vulgar cypresses, but there were no trees whatsoever, unless you count the stunted wind-blown ones planted right next to Max's house. They were the nurselings of the poet's late mother, Elena (called Pra by the family). How happy she would have felt if she had the opportunity to see the dense park which now surrounds the house. When I look at a recent picture of the poet's home buried in greenery I cannot help thinking it a miracle.

So we looked around us; no bright colors, everything was reddish-gray. "A primitive beauty," as Maximilian expressed it. How he loved this little corner of the Crimea! And yet he had travelled quite extensively in the world and seen quite a lot of beauty both at home and abroad. Here he is in his study with the windows overlooking the sea (and just think—there's never any dust).

He reads poetry.

> *With old gold and bile*
> *The evening light nurtures the hills.*
> *Fading are the reds and browns of the*
> *Clumps of shaggy grass like the strands of red fur.*
> *In the fire the shrubbery and water are like metal.*
>   (From the cycle "Cimmerian Twilights")

We listen, —Anna Ostroumova-Levedeva, Dora Karmen, the mother of the well-known film-maker, Olga Golovina, myself and somebody else whom I do not remember. But I did not see Leonev, Shengeli, Sofia Fedorenko or M.A. at these readings.

This brings to mind the fact that M.A. was not particularly drawn to poetry, although he understood perfectly well what was good and what was bad, and could himself resort to verse on occasion. I remember one time at the Lyamins' when M.A. took a little book by a contemporary poet and read a poem first as it was printed, from the top to the bottom, and then from the bottom upwards. And the meaning of the poem was about the same.

"You see, Kolya, it turns out that this poet is not a poet at all," he said.

When I woke up early at Koktebel, I was afraid that since it was cloudy, the weather would be bad, but it was the fog coming in from the sea. Around ten o'clock the cloud cover had dispersed and a cloudless day set in. A long summer's day.

Like everybody else we caught the "stone disease" so typical of Koktebel. We collected pebbles in our pockets and handkerchiefs, regarded them as "the glory of creation" because of their beauty and then dumped out our booty in front of Max, but he would say with a good-natured smile:

"The most common dogs!"

The lowest class was dogs, the higher one was frogs and the highest one was carnelian.

We walked to Kara-Dag. Maximilian walked in front stepping unusually lightly. All of us were panting and dripping with sweat but Max strode off as if nothing was the matter, and the heat was nothing to him. When I expressed surprise, he explained to me that in his youth he had gone all over Central Asia with a caravan.

Kara-Dag is an extinct volcano. It was a splendid and moving sight. There was hardened lava in the crater—there was an illusion that it was Notre Dame de Paris. How sweetly one was drawn to this scenic abyss!

"Now this is really vertigo," M.A. explained to me as he pulled me away from the edge.

He did not especially care for long excursions. Other than the walk to Kara-Dag, we took walks along the beach and swam occasionally as the need arose. But the most entertaining occupation was to catch butterflies. Marya provided us with nets.

Here we are clambering up a nearby hill and then the fun begins. M.A. had the pink sunburn of the light-skinned blonds. His eyes seemed especially sky-blue because of his bright color and from the blue cap also given to him by Marya.

He yells:

"Hold it! Catch him! That's a 'satyr.' " I swing the net but not in the right place. It is really slippery in the dry grass, which is on the slope. I slide downward. I see how M.A. slides down on his belly on the other side. Both of us laugh. But the "satyrs" flutter about us without a care in the world.

Later M.A.'s sister Nadezhda told me that at one time during his student years her brother had had a passion for butterflies and that his collection was eventually given to Kiev University.

Exhausted, we go swimming. During the hottest time of the day, everyone goes and hides in their rooms. There are no trees, of course, and that means no shade. It is not hot in our room, it smells of wormwood from the fresh twigs that I sweep out our room with.

Anna Ostroumova-Lebedeva expressed the desire to do a water color portrait of M.A.

He poses for her in that same hat with blue piping that was decorated with Koktebel pebbles. I remember liking the portrait then.

In 1968 I was able to see it again after an interval of several decades, and I was surprised that I could have liked it so much. Several times during the sittings Anna, who was a good storyteller, mentioned the poet Briusov. He had told her that he had half-opened the curtain to the next world and had delved into its depths when he was studying the occult sciences. But woe to the uninitiated—he proclaimed—who dare to encroach upon those depths without being prepared for it... I admit that I could not listen to Anna without gasping. M.A. held his peace. And today I am reading Ehrenburg's book *People, Years, Life* (v. 1-2, p. 365) and I read: "Surrounded by poets and in the grip of mystical moods he (Briusov—L.B.) started to study 'the occult sciences' and knew all the peculiarities of incubus and succubus, exorcism and the medieval soothsaying." And those distant conversations during the sittings acquire another color and another sense. Involuntarily one recalls Briusov's "The Fiery Angel."

In the female population of Voloshin's house Natalia Gabrichevsky played first fiddle. Her appearance was flashy: smooth, suntanned skin, a face with beautiful color, eyes which are large and prominent, and her eyebrows are drawn in. There is a bright ribbon around her head. She loves to sing racy little ditties; I sometimes hear an outburst of male laughter from the corner of the bottom floor where the Gabrichevskys live.. She treats women of a different type with a light contempt, and calls them—me, for instance—"a little lady with flowers." Only once, and not for long, did she and I get together. At a Tatar holiday (Bairam or Ramadan) in Upper or Lower Otuzy (I no longer remember which) the two of us, dressed in Tatar costume, danced the "kaytarma" (and we danced it badly)... But it simply would not be fair to mention Natalia of those years and not throw a bridge across the years to today.

In March 1968, I was at an exhibition of her pictures. However strange it may sound, there had "erupted" in her when she was elderly, talent as an artist.

I can confidently use that responsible word because her drawings are really talented—sharply satirical, drawn in a decorative primitive style. I liked best an oil portrait of the actor Rumnev. He is pictured in a pink shirt and a round straw hat, the brim of which does not fit in the frame of the picture. Whether because the hat was reminiscent of the solar disk or that there is not a single touch of shade in the picture, I was overcome by the sensation of a hot summer's day.

Her husband, Alexander, an art critic, and admirer of beauty, could praise the architectonics of any little gray Crimean prickly burr, admiringly turning it around and rolling his r-s all the time with pure French refinement.

In the gallery of French painting in the Pushkin Museum of Fine Arts there is a marble sculpture by Rodin, of an immense male head with an abundant crop of hair. This is a bust of Georgi Gabrichevsky, a doctor and one of the founders of Russian microbiology.

Gabrichevsky Junior did not look at all like the marble portrait of his father. He was a little bald and pudgy in spite of his young age—he was then about 32-33 years old.

We had already met this couple at the Lyamins.

All of us lived in harmony, for the most part. If there were no especially close bonds of friendship, then there was also no mutual backbiting. The Voloshin couple behaved very tactfully; they were uniformly friendly to all.

Once Maximilian came up to M.A. and said that the writer Alexander Grin wanted to meet him. He was then living at Feodosia and would be at Koktebel on an appointed day. And then there arrived a sun-bronzed, strong, no longer young man in a white tunic and white service cap looking like the captain of a large river steamer. His eyes were dark and melancholy like Mayakovsky's eyes, and the heavy features of his face were also reminiscent of the poet. With him came a very attractive, impressive woman with light brown hair and a light-colored lace scarf. Grin introduced her as his wife. As far as I remember, the conversation didn't take. I discovered a trait in M.A. which came out very clearly in those days—he felt considerably more at ease when talking to women. I examined the sunburned "captain" with curiosity and thought: truly, there is no prophet in his own land. Before me was a wizard of a writer whose works were suffused with the fragrance of distant and fantastic lands. He was an intriguing and rare phenomenon in our "established" literature, but he enjoyed no real appreciation or success during those years. We went to see them off. They left early since they were walking. As we were parting Alexander smiled his nice smile and asked us to come and visit them:

"We will treat you to some delicious pies!" And the impressive one confirmed it: "We will definitely give you some."

But we left without having seen Grin a second time (which I regret to this day). If the writer Sofia Fedorchenko—a curious woman—had not been sick she might have shown some interest in going to visit Grin. But she became ill, and lay in her room, fussing and tormenting her selfless husband Nikolai.

Nor did the other inhabitants of Voloshin's household show any particular interest in going.

The handsome head of Yuri Slezkin appeared briefly on our Koktebel horizon and then disappeared...

Voloshin's love for Koktebel was gradually and imperceptibly beginning to infect me. I was already delighted with the red hills and loved to hear Max's poem about the place.

But M.A. remained firm in his dislike for the Crimea. I have a letter from him written five years later in which he writes: "The Crimea is, as always, a little repulsive..." But during more than eight years of living together we nevertheless travelled to the Crimea three times: to Koktebel, Miskhor and Sudak, and on the way we stopped to look at Alupka, Feodosia, Yalta, Sevastopol... The days flew by and we had to leave.

Feodosia again.

Before the steamer left we went to the Aivazovsky Museum and both of us were surprised to discover that he was such an excellent portrait painter... M.A. said that one should eat heartily in order to avoid getting seasick. We went to the dining room on the steamer. The steamer was starting to rock slightly while still at the mooring. A young woman with a baby came in and sat down at the table. Then she suddenly turned pale, stuck the swaddled baby into the corner of the sofa and staggered towards the door.

"It's starting," said M.A. ominously.

The whistle sounded for the departure. We went out on deck.

Over the sides of the boat gray waves were rolling in humps. It was raining. M.A. said, "If it rocks from fore to aft you must look at this point. But if it rolls from side to side you must look over there."

"Oh, what a sea-wolf you are! I'll have no trouble if I'm with you," I said and started to walk around the steamer. Many people were already lying down. I felt fine and put myself at the disposal of the captain's assistant who was plump and pink and had a shiny pimple on his forehead. He shouted: "You there in yellow! (I was wearing a yellow dress.) Some water over here! You in yellow, hurry up!"

And so on.

There were some funny moments too. An elderly woman was lying on the floor right in the passage way. The captain's assistant grabbed her under the arms and I by the legs to free the passage. The woman opened her glazed eyes and said beseechingly:

"Don't throw me in the sea!"

"We won't throw you in, mama, we won't throw you in!" said the assistant soothingly.

I went to look for my "sea-wolf." He was sitting where I had left him.

"Look, Maka dear," I said tenderly, leaning on his shoulder. "Look, look, we are passing Kara-Dag."

He turned his unhappy face to me and articulated with a

voice that came from deep inside him,

"Don't lean on your elbows or I'll throw up!"

This phrase later found its way, with a few changes, into the mouth of Lariosik in *The Days of the Turbins*:

"Don't kiss, or I'll throw up!"

When we arrived at Yalta the lights were on in the city—it was very beautiful—and strangely enough we got settled immediately in a hotel without having to walk around looking for shelter for the night, and pay two rubles per bed at Aunt Dasha's or Aunt Pasha's, as is done nowadays.

In the morning we went to Sevastopol. We did not struggle with the tickets, the porter took them. We admired the view over the harbor and the city.

There appeared later in *The Red Evening Gazette* (1925) a series of feuilletons by M.A. Bulgakov about the Crimea.

And even later there was an echo of the Crimea when a lady showed up at our "Dovecote" wearing a large black hat decorated with pebbles from Koktebel. Their weight bent the lady's head now to the right, now to the left, but she resolutely regained her balance. The visitor conveyed greetings from Max and delivered some of his watercolors as a gift. There was a note on one of them in Voloshin's tiny handwriting referring to *White Guard*: "To the first to imprint the soul of the Russian internal strife."

We also received a visit from M.A.'s sister Varvara, who is described in the novel *The White Guard* (Elena), and from there she migrated to the play *The Days of the Turbins*. She was a sweet-looking woman with a heavy lower jaw. She behaved like an incensed princess; she was offended on behalf of her husband who is very negatively described in the novel *White Guard* under the name of Talberg. She left without saying two words to me. M.A. was embarrassed...

I remember one of the first "slaps in the face" (there were countless ones later). This is how Viktor Shklovsky expressed himself in one of his works: "Bulgakov is on the mat."(*Gamburgskii schet*, Leningrad, 1928, p. 5) I will explain this to those who are not familiar with this expression. It refers to the fact that clowns entertain the public by performing on a mat in the circus ring.

I will never forget how M.A.'s face quivered and how pale

he became. Shklovsky's attack was so much more difficult to understand since he had just consulted Bulgakov a few days earlier to get some medical advice. It was, of course, impossible to become completely immune to slaps in the face and to needling, but it was really necessary to cover oneself with thicker skin, as life itself would prove.

In the meantime work on the play *The Days of the Turbins* was progressing. You might call this period in M.A.'s life the dawn of his relationship with the Art Theater. And of course there was no way to foresee that in about ten years this bright love affair with the theater would be transformed into *Theatrical Novel*, also known as *Black Snow*. M.A. was at that time ecstatic about the theater. And if Glinka said: "Music is my soul" then Bulgakov might have said, "The theater is my soul."

I remember that he hesitated when K.S. Stanislavsky advised him to combine Colonel Nai-Turs and Aleksei Turbin into one character in order to strengthen the artistic effect. The author regretted parting with Nai-Turs, but he understood that Stanislavsky was right.

As far as I can remember, the production of *The Days of the Turbins* underwent several changes. I remember the first version on stage with a scene showing the anti-Bolshevik Cossacks at the staff head-quarters of Bolbotun's First Cavalry Division. At first a deserter with frost-bitten feet comes to the front of the stage, then the shoemaker with a basket of his wares, and then an old Jew. The Cossack Lieutenant Galanba is interrogating them; he is a dapper coldblooded murderer (Maloletkov played him—he was good). The shoemaker was played very well by Blinnikov. The Jew was played equally well by Raevsky. Lieutenant Galanba kills him. It is a terrible scene. At this dress rehearsal I sat beside K.S. Stanislavsky. He turned his silvery head to me and said: "Those scoundrels cut out this scene." (That is how he unflatteringly referred to the Central Repertory Committee). I replied hoarsely "Yes." (I had lost my voice from agitation). The scene was not retained in this form. The scene at the home of the housing manager Lisovich, "At Vasilisa's," was also included at this dress rehearsal. Vasilisa was played by Tarkhanov and his wife Wanda was played by Anastasia Zueva. The two profiteers were hiding their valuables in a secret hiding place, but they were watched by bandits who robbed them of everything they had. In spite of the excellent acting the scene was considered to be irrelevant, not fitting into the fabric of the play and making the performance drag, and Stanislavsky took it out.

Muscovites know how successful the play was. One of our acquaintances saw a particular performance when a characteristic event occurred.

It was during the third act of *The Days of the Turbins*. The battalion had been defeated. The city was taken by the Gaidamak Cossacks. It is a tense moment. The dawn can be seen through the Turbins' window. Elena and Lariosik are waiting. And suddenly a faint knock... Both of them listen attentively... Unexpectedly an agitated female voice is heard from the audience: "Open up—it's all right! It's one of ours!" That was a merging of theater and life that playwrights, actors, and directors can only hope for.

On the tennis court at Kriukovo. Left to right: A. Ponsov, L. E. Bulgakova, D. Ponsov, M. A. Bulgakov, N. Lyamin, N. Nikitinsky, S. Topleninov.

NO. 4 MALY LEVSHINSKY STREET

We moved. We had two small rooms (two!), and although we shared the hall we had our own door. The building was one of a million ordinary Moscow houses. At one time the masters of the mansion had lived there and received visitors, sending the children either to the back rooms or to the second floor, with their governesses if they were wealthy, or with their nannies if they were less wealthy. And now we moved in where the nannies used to live.

We slept in the blue room and spent the day in the yellow one. The fashion then was to paint the walls with glossy paint in the colors that were used in the 1840s and 1850s.

We shared a kitchen without gas; primus stoves hummed on the tables and kerosine lamps blinked. The house was spacious but crammed to overflowing. Just who didn't live here? A couple of students, a typesetter, an engineer, office workers, housewives, a seamstress and various children. Especially numerous were the children in the engineer's family—or so it seemed. His mother-in-law, a respectable and cultured woman, was a relative of Vasily Zhukovsky through his beloved niece Moyer,* on which subject she gave us an essay to read.

A fixture in the kitchen was a gray cat who could shoot up to the window vent like a whirlwind without forgetting to nibble at the caviar on the primus stove on his way up.

The window in the yellow room was wide. I had long dreamed of an Italian window. Soon a box appeared on the windowsill, and in the box nasturtiums. Macka immediately composed these lines:

> *In the chamberpot, why—God knows,*
> *Some doleful, clinging, green weed grows.*
> *It seems that the conclusion is*
> *Some barefoot tramp made this house his.*

The phrase "barefoot tramp" is from Southern Russia and is one of Bulgakov's favorite terms. Many expressions and proverbs of their own invention were always going around in his

---

*Marie Moyer, née Protasov, died in 1823 (tr.)

family. If someone (and there were seven children) had to get up from the table when there was something good on it, he would ask his neighbor: "Guard it!"

This whole team (a close knit one, I must say) grew up together, went to school together, joked, quarreled, made up, and laughed together.

When the team grew up, the mischief assumed new forms and the subject matter broadened. During their youth they even parodied the poet Nikitin:

Mother lay down and prayed in God's name;
The children sat down and played a card game.

A sense of humor, wit, the ability to support each other, fortitude; all these qualities are to be found in a family with good mettle. This mettle was a great support to Bulgakov during a period of especially severe persecution.

Our house was on the corner of Maly Levshinsky Street and on the other side it faced No. 30, Prechistenka (now Kropotinskaya). I remember the sign over the gate: "Exempt from billeting" written in the old orthography. It seemed so old-fashioned... The delightful thing about our new home was that all our friends lived in the same area. We only needed to cross the street, follow the perpendicular lane, and we were at the Lyamins!

Even nearer, on Mansurovsky Lane, lived Seryozha Topleninov, a charming and companionable man who was a jack-of-all-trades. He played the guitar and was an expert on old romances.

The Moritses lived on Pomerantsev Lane, and, on our own Maly Levshinsky street, Vladimir Dolgoruky (Vladimirov) lived. He was our "court poet" V.D., of whom Maka wrote in his diary: "Remind Lyubasha not to forget to get mad at V.D."

The fact was that Vladimir had written poetry dedicated to Maka, me, and our cats. Tatyana Lyamin and Seryozha Topleninov illustrated the book. There was also a portrait of V.D. in it. He asked permission to take the little book home with him, and promised not to touch any of the pictures. But he did not keep his promise; he retouched his portrait which made me justifiably angry.

Just a few steps across Ostozhenka (now Metrostroevskaya) lived the two Nikitinskys, Kolya Lyamin's cousins.

In the basement of the Tolstoy Museum lived the writer Sofya Fedorchenko and her husband Nikolai Rakitsky. That was five minutes from our house, and we sometimes dropped in there for a cup of tea. I recall one particular evening. We dropped in at Sofya Fedorchenko's on our way home. A dusky, dark-haired young man was sitting at the table.

After tea Sofya said, "Please Boris, you wanted to read your poetry." Pasternak (it was he) straightened himself up a little and leaning back in his chair a bit, he started to recite:

> *The sun set*
> *And suddenly*
> *The Potemkin blazed up with electricity.*
> *From the galley to the spardeck*
> *A mass of flies swooped in.*
> *The meat was a bit off...*
> *And darkness fell over the sea.*
> *The light grumbled till dawn*
> *And after barely gleaming in the morning, it went*
> *out...*

I am not going to say that I particularly liked the poem, but the words "The light grumbled till dawn" (or "The world grumbled till dawn") confused both M.A. and me. We even decided that we had not heard it right. On the other hand the poet's looks made an impression on me: there was something Eastern and ecstatic in his whole appearance, in his dark lusterless eyes, and in his hoarse voice. It seemed that if he had swayed slightly back and forth and fingered some beads while he was reading, he would have looked like and inspired Arab. But he sat straight upright, and he did not have any beads...

At the intersection of the two lanes—Maly and Bolshoi Levshinsky—there was a white toy-like church with blue cupolas decorated with stars. M.A.'s younger sister Leyla Bulgakova married Mikhail Svetlaev there. She looked very sweet in her wedding gown.

In the spring M.A. and I travelled to Miskhor; from the Resort Administration we rented one room for us and another for the two Svetlaevs in a dacha which formerly belonged to Chichkin... What old Muscovite does not recognize this dairy name? On every corner there used to be a sign with clearly visible letters: Chichkin.

We liked the dacha very much. It was a spacious and well built house by the sea without any merchant-like extravagance. A doctor from the Resort Administration who had been negotiating with us complained over some administrative problem and said, "And here I stand between Scylla and Charbydis." The latter name became his nickname and we already spoke of him in feminine genter: "Charbydis, she came, Charbydis, she said..."

I remember walking along the path around our house one morning. Our neighbors, man and wife, were standing at the window. M.A. said very politely, as always: "Good morning to you, comrades!" to which they replied: "To some a comrade, to some a gray wolf." Later on it got even more interesting. We had to take our meals at the neighboring dacha, which used to be the castle of some former Grand Duke. The tables stood on a large terrace. One time after the regular meal, somebody asked Bulgakov to explain what is meant by a woman of "Balzacian age." He began to explain that in the novel a thirty-year old woman chose a lover who was much younger than herself, and he gave an example for the sake of clarity: "Let us suppose that Olga Knipper-Chekhova fell in love with a member of the Komsomol..." He had barely uttered the last word when some creature, pale with emotion, shouted: "Comrades! You hear how he makes fun of the Komsomol. He wants to degrade the Komsomol! We will not stand for such an outrage!"

Then I delivered my "speech from the throne." I said that M.A. did not wish to offend anybody, that there was some misunderstanding here and so on, but the hysterical woman kept raging until a handsome Armenian in her party took her arm and led her down a nearby lane where he walked her around for a long time and rebuked her softly, "One has to be tolerant, there's no need to make a mountain out of a molehill..."

This unexpectedly stormy outburst forced us to be careful, to avoid the word "comrade" and to avoid as far as possible discussions of literary subjects. In the evenings now when croquet games were arranged we (Maka, Lelya Svetlaev and I) tried not to lose, because our opponents tried to hit our balls and then knock them far over the precipice down to the sea, which we were too gentlemanly to permit ourselves to do. You had to go down and get the balls, which meant that you also had to climb back up the tiring and steep rocky path. All in all, after a month's worth of the Crimea, we were homesick.

Somewhat disappointed we returned home and immediately started thinking about what to do with the rest of the summer; and then we heard from the Lyamins that their relatives the Nikitinskys were living in Kryukov near Moscow, in the Ponsov dacha (an old Muscovite family), and that they were very contented. We went there on a reconnaissance trip. We liked it too. Moreover, it was bliss not to have to do any planning.

We could not really believe at first how many people were living in that spacious house. The only thing to do after getting used to it was to count everybody. I will start with the masters of the house—Lidya, a beautiful and striking woman, the head, brain and heart of the whole clan. Her husband Dmitri was, as they say, a smart operator; and he was, for the most part, in town, busy with his affairs. The two of them, both husband and wife, behaved wisely, not taking any part in our amusements although they were invariably spectators at all our performances.

There were three daughters; the eldest, Evgenya, was a reserved and well brought up girl. She was married to a nice, tall, half-blind man, Fyodor Malinin. I took a really close look at Evgenya on the tennis court. She looke unusually elegant and fragile, and it was strange to see her hit the balls with a strong masculine swing.

The second sister was Lidya. She was an attractive, statuesque, well-built girl, a Juno with a light tread and an easy laugh which she was able to preserve throughout her life. Lidya was hospitality and comfort personified.

The youngest specimen was Elena. I say "specimen" on purpose because that is exactly what she was. She was homely, witty, talented, and an excellent story-teller; she worked for many years at the Vakhtangov Theater and died with the title of People's Artist of the Russian Federation. At that time, in 1926, she had just started at the theater and had as yet played only one role, the old woman in Seifullina's *Virineya*.

When Lenka (that is what she was called at home) was in form, she could have amused even the "Princess who couldn't laugh." Sometimes she was overcome by a desire to dance. She improvised to the sounds of the piano, and quite well, too.

There were also two brothers; Georges, who was grown up and married, and Alyosha, a boy of seven or eight.

I have enumerated the Ponsov family who lived on the bottom floor of the house. Georges and his wife Katya and their little son lived in the wing. Elena and Ivan Nikitinsky and their two-year-old son and nanny lived on the top floor. The Nikitinskys' great friend, the artist Seryozha Topleninov, was staying there as a guest. They gave us a room that was added to the house and had a separate entrance. This was especially delightful in case of after-hours get-togethers. And we did have some of those; several times we stayed up until very late.

I will just mention the kaleidoscope of guests. There were people who did not live in the villa but who came almost every day (the four Dobrynins, their cousin M.G. Nesterenko, who lived next-door to them and who was nicknamed "Little Tomato" because of his round shape and rosy cheeks); there were occasional guests (the artist Vsevolod Verbitsky of the Moscow Art Theater, the first-class tennis player Maltseva, Ruben Simonov, A.A. Orochko, V. Lvova and many others): and there were regular guests who came to spend week-ends (Shura and Volodya Morits). The center of activities, meetings, and conversations was the tennis court and the benches beside it under the birch trees. The games were serious business to Zhenya, Vsevolod Verbitsky and Ruben Simonov, who was at that time thin and very active. When he returned the ball he raised his leg like a goat and let out peals of laughter. The participants in the game would vary. M.A. once boasted that he could beat everybody if he wanted to, but he was quickly "unmasked." Lidya accused him of holding the racket "like a paddle," that is so that it stands perpendicular to the hand instead of serving as an extension of the hand. I often heard Lidya's voice, "Maka, you are holding the racket like a paddle again!" But once he showed class; he fell, but managed even to return a difficult shot.

All of us loved Petya Vasilyev, a neighbor who came almost every day. He was a good-natured and pleasant fat man who was also a strong-man. Seryozha Topleninov drew a caricature of him which resembled him very much. In the heat Petya's hair curled up especially tightly; in the country they say about such hair that "you cannot break it with a whip." When he hit the ball back or tried to do so he used to laught in a different sort of way, and if he missed he would exclaim in German: "Es ist ja ganz verdriesslich," which means "But this is quite annoying."

In the evenings everybody gathered in the living room. The kerosine lamp burned cozily under the lampshade—there was no electricity. The center of things here was the piano at which Zhenya (a good musician) or the composer Nikolai Sizov, who was renting a room in the village, would sit down. He had the habit of appearing suddenly—like a thief in the night—and then disappearing as suddenly. People often asked: "Have you seen Nikolai?" The answer was: "Yes, he was here just now. Where can he have gone?" But he sat down at the instrument without being asked when Lidya wanted to sing a French song with her silvery voice, or if we needed musical accompaniment to play charades, or if we simply felt like dancing.

One time Petya performed what is called a "strong-man act" at the circus. He lay face down on the divan and asked all of us to lie down on top, which we were glad to do. A small mound was formed. Petya waited a little, strained and, supporting himself on the divan with his hands he got up and threw all of us on the floor. Maka said: "You think that's hard?"

He lay face down on the divan and all of us merrily piled ourselves on top of him. After a couple of seconds he turned his pale face toward us(I will never forget how he looked) and uttered with a feeble voice: "Get off me as quickly as possible."

At once we rolled off him like peas. "The strong-man act" did not come off, but M.A. performed other, more successful acts. At charades he was the greatest. There he is with a sponge mop on his head representing gray hair and conducting an invisible orchestra. He always did love to conduct. Sometimes he took a pencil and reproduced a conductor's movements— he was deeply impressed by this profession, in fact, it attracted him. This was the famous conductor of the Bolshoi Theater, Suk* (the first syllable of the charade).

---

*Vyacheslav Ivanovich Suk, 1861-1933. (tr.)

Then two people (Lidya and "Little Tomato") play tennis right there in the living room. You can hear "out," "in," "serving." All of the scoring for this game and all the customary terms are breezily pronounced in English by the Dobrynins. ("In" is the second syllable of the charade.) The third one is "son." The return of the prodigal son. And all of it together, the wonderful shaggy dog Buyan comes in from the terrace, squinting confused in the light. He is a "son of a bitch."*

I no longer remember the charade where Maka played alady in Lidya Mitrofanovna's dressing gown with blue and white stripes. He was particularly funny when at the end of his performance he matter-of-factly threw away his bust—the sofa-pillows. M.A. invented one other game. All divided into two groups. The participants hold on the edge of a sheet and stretch it out at face level. You put a light tuft of fluffy cotton in the center of the sheet. Now everybody starts blowing, trying to drive it towards the opposing team. The losers have to pay a forfeit... The contest was noisy and a lot of fun.

Who first came up with the idea to have a spiritualistic seance is now hard to say. I think it was Seryozha Topleninov. At any rate, M.A. warmly supported this suggestion. We sat down around a circular table, placed our hands on the top of the table forming a chain, and then we elected the one who was to contact the spirit—Seryozha Topleninov. We put out the light. In the ensuing darkness and silence Seryozha's solemn and slightly funereal voice resounded, "Spirit, if you are here, manifest yourself in some way."

One moment went by...the table began to tremble and started to tear itself away from our hands. Seryozha quieted it down with difficulty, and silence again ensued.

"Let some object fly about the room if you are here," said our medium. And immediately a book flew rustling across the room into a corner. The atmosphere rose to fever pitch. After a minute Vanya Nikitinsky gave a shout, "Turn on the light! He touched me on the head! Light!"

"Ouch, me too!"

Now one of the women shouted, "Seryozha, tell him not to touch me!"

---

*The Russian for "son of a bitch" is "sukin syn."(tr.)

The spirit pulled one hairpin out of Zhenya's hairdo and threw it on the table. And the other one. There were shrieks here and there. The lamp was lit. All were dishevelled and agitated. We told each other about the sensations we had had. The medium triumphed; the seance had been a glorious success. Some scepticism was expressed, but rather feebly.

Next morning the discussion continued. Elena Ponsova said, "This is not a vacation cottage—damned if I know what it is! Today I was (she performs a mime), tomorrow I iron (another pantomime) and I am going to walk to Moscow on the railroad bed (the funniest performance of all)."

In the morning, however, our "truth lover" Elena Nikitinskaya waylaid Petya Vasilev in the hall and started trying to get him to tell the truth; did he have anything to do with the manifestation of the spirit the day before?

"What is the matter with you, Elena?"

But she insisted, "Give me your word, Petya!"

"I give you my word."

"Swear by your grandmother (she was the only one in his family that she knew)."

And then you could hear Petya's thick deceitful voice, "I swear by my grandmother!"

M.A. and I swore by grandmother for a long time after that when we fibbed...

The excitement did not die down. The mistress of the house, Lidya, called me into her and asked me what had really happened.

I had no answer yet.

The second seance took place with the participation of the Vakhtangov actors, who shrugged their shoulders but condescended to take part anyway. The manifestations were repeated; but this time radishes flew onto the table, and we ate them for supper. In this way we demonstrated a direct link between the incorporeal spirit and bodily nourishment... Later I accidentally overheard a conversation between the two conspirators, Maka and Petya,

"Petya, you damned dog, why did you throw the radish on the table?"

"I had to use whatever I could lay my hands on, Maka," he justified himself.

"Aha! I just knew that you two were cheating."

The two of them stopped and M.A. tried to bribe me (not very generously: he offered me three rubles to keep quiet). But I behaved like the incorruptible Robespierre and demanded nothing less than full disclosure. It was a simple matter. Petya sat down beside M.A. and let go of M.A.'s right hand, thereby freeing his own left hand. Beforehand Maka had hidden a switch with the tip bent under his jacket. He touched bald and not so bald heads with it and brought terror to the participants in the seance.

If I had had black gloves, he said to me later, I could have driven everybody out of their minds...

Among our amusements there was no communal singing. Except perhaps that we sang "Kambambully" now and then. It was mostly Seryozha Topleninov who sang to the guitar: "I met you," "The shadows drift together," "The garden gate," "We went out into the garden" and many other nice songs. I remember one more old song: "Say a word for the poor hussar, your husband won't let him spend the night here, but a woman's heart is kinder than a man's and will surely take pity on me..."

Our peaceful life was disturbed by the rumors that the place was infested with criminals who had escaped from the nearby prison camp. And unfortunately the rumors were in fact confirmed. Not far from where Petya lived a whole family of five was butchered. Later the pharmacist in the village by Kryukov station was shot.

Once during the night when almost everybody was asleep a woman's shriek was heard from the neighboring dacha:

"Watchman! Help! Help!"

A terrible turmoil ensued. All jumped out of their beds just as they were. Georges ran out with a gun and fired a couple of times in the air. The dogs that I was taking care of, Vertushka and Buyan, hid trembling under the table on the terrace.

Seryozha was in bed in the Nikitinskys' room but was not asleep yet. Lena asked him, "Seryozha, did you hear?"

He replied, "Yes. I am reading *Anna Karenina*."

Vanya was standing on the stairs by the door ready to defend his family. He stood there in nothing but his underwear, a coat and cap on his head. He held a heavy chandelier in his hands.

In spite of the alarming situation—a person crying, a person running, a person firing a gun—my knees were shaking from laughter when I looked at this knight in his shorts.

Luckily, Petya was spending the night in the villa, and he took his revolver and went next door. It turned out that there was no bandit there. It was simply a cat who jumped from the roof to a lower roof. Of course, when the cat ran across the tin roof, he had made a noise which was emphasized and strengthened by the quiet of the night, but the tense nerves of the inhabitants did not continue. In the morning everybody laughed at each other, our faces still showing what had taken place. And once again, we began to live quietly and enjoy the summer that continued to be marvellously clear and fragrant.

Those of us who are still living remember how we lived at Kryukov. The secret of the persistence of those memories lies in the unusually benevolent atmosphere that prevailed during those days. There was some sort of guarantee of mutual sympathy and confidence... How nice it is when everyone wishes everyone else well!

Now that I have told about the summer at Kryukov, I would like to mention the late Georges Ponsov. During his last years he suffered from tuberculosis and could no longer work: his wife Katya did work. The son was growing up, and of course it was no easy life for them. Because of her work, Katya had to be away from Moscow. Then Georges became very sick, but he refused to alarm his wife. With his last strength he wrote her several letters "in advance," so to speak, and have them to a friend to send to Katya after he was no longer among the living. The friend followed his instructions. Poor Georges! What was he feeling while he was writing those letters... I do not know of anyone or have even heard of anyone else capable of showing such delicate feelings, and in literature I know only one story, "Tenderness," by Henri Barbusse, where the story is reminiscent of Georges' action. But the heroine in the story commits suicide, and her beloved, who does not know about her death, now and then receives her letters filled with warmth and love, which are sent by a faithful friend.

It is 1927. With his leg tucked under him (a family habit: M.A.'s sister Nadezhda also likes to sit that way) and with candles burning, Bulgakov usually sits and writes during the night. In the daytime he sometimes reads bits of some scene or other from *The*

Crimson Island or repeats some phrase from it that especially pleases him. "Horrors, horrors, horrors, horrors," he often says like the adventurer and upstart Kiri-Kuki in that play. The kaleidoscopic nature of the plot amuses him. Jules Verne's heroes, who are also the characters in the play, are well known and loved by him since the days of his youth, but his brilliant memory and imagination bring their characters to life in unfading colors.

The fight between the white Arabs and the Red Natives on the Crimson Island is only froth, lace, and a background activity. The essence of the play, its fundamental meaning, lies in the fate of the young writer, in his creative dependence on the "sinister old man," the censor Savva Lukich.

I remember that there was a lot of music, movement, and authorial mischief on stage. Ryndin's scenery was good and as always at the Kamerny Theater, the lighting was worked out especially carefully.

I recall the actor Ganshin in the role of the writer. Savva Lukich was made up to look like Blyum, who worked at Main Repertory Committee (the censorship board), and he was one of the most vicious persecutors of Bulgakov.*

I can remember how an usher at the theater came up on stage and announced respectfully and triumphantly, "Savva Lukich is removing his galoshes in the lobby!"

He was proud to perform at the theater. And his words resounded like an incantation with increasing strength from the orchestra to the prompter's box and from the prompter's box onto the stage, "Savva Lukich is removing his galoshes in the lobby!" Even the sailors on the ship are announcing it. The theater director who played the lord said, clutching his head, "I hear you, I hear you. All right, receive, call, ask, tell that I am very happy..."

Fear and agitation made him slip into the role of Famusov in Griboedov's *Woe From Wit*.

In the epilogue the sinister Savva addresses the author: "Of course, I'm still banning your little play for all other cities... it's impossible... a play like that to be suddenly passed for everywhere!"

---

*Blyum, Vladimir. Censor and drama critic who wrote under the pseudonym of "Sadko."

The Crimson Island was produced by A.Ya. Tairov at the Kamerny Theater in 1928. The play was very successful but was soon removed from the repertory...

His intoxication with tht theater continues. *The Turbins* is playing with unchanging success. The actors play unusually well together and for this reason they themselves call the show a "concert."

The question of a banquet came up. Vladimir Stepun, an actor from the Art Theater, who was in the play, came to the rescue. He offered his own apartment at 41 Sivtsev-Vrazhek. The most difficult role was not just to accomodate everybody, set the table and serve forty persons, but to arrange the food attractively and to clean up afterwards. This role was taken on by Vladimir's wife Yulia Lvovna, the daughter of Professor Tarasevich. Extremely long tables were being set in large rooms on the ground floor, facing the courtyard of No. 41.

It became my responsibility to see to the food and wine. Petya Vasilev came to my assistance. The Hunters' Market fortunately still existed in the center of Moscow. This was a marvellous venture. We hired a cab and took a look at all the shops one after the other. There were many different kinds of caviar, smoked sturgeon, white salmon, plain sturgeon, plain salmon and stellate sturgeon in one place; barrels of different pickles, mushrooms and cucumbers in another place, and game and sausages in a third one. The wine was in a fourth place. We ordered pies and cakes from an efficient private baker on Stoleshnikov Lane. Then we brought everything to the nice Stepuns',

I will give some of the names of the banquet participants according to M.A.'s own note which I found at the house of his sister Nadezhda Zemskaya:

Maloletkov	Khmelev
Ershov	Kaluzhsky
Novikov	Mitropolsky
Anders	
Butyugin	
Guzeev	
Lifanov	
Aksenov	
Dobronravov	

Lyamin—two
Three Ponsov Sisters
Vera Sokolova
Wanda Fedorova
Stepun—two
Mordvinov
Istrin
Mikhalsky
Yanshin

Wanda Fedorova was an attractive woman. She worked at the Art Theater. Her husband, Vladimir used to come to play whist with us. M.A. frequently visited that hospitable family, and sometimes I went along with him.

I did not find the names of Pavel Markov and Ilya Sudakov, the director of the play, on the list.

All night long we had fun, singing and dancing.

That evening Lena Ponsova and Viktor Stanitsyn exchanged very special glances (they soon got married).

I remember that it was already morning when Lidya danced through the entire "Russian Dance" with Maloletkov as partner in the courtyard. Of course, M.A. and I were very grateful to the Stepun family for having very kindly taken on so much fuss and bother.

While speaking of *The Days of the Turbins* it would also be appropriate to mention the first criticism of the play. One day a gloomy young man in glasses showed up at our place; we did not know him. It was Levushka Ostroumov (as the Lyamins told us later), and he gave M.A. a dressing-down. The play was badly written, he said, and the classical canons were not observed in it. He grumbled in a hostile way for a long time and mentioned Aristotle frequently. M.A. did not say a word. Then the critic left with the wrong galoshes...

Somewhat later the critic Sadko raged in his article "The Beginning of the End of the Moscow Art Theater" (*Art Life*, Vol. 43, 1927) in connection with the renewal of the play *The Days of the Turbins*. He called Bulgakov "the prophet and apostle of Russian Philistinism" (p.7) and the play itself "the most trivial play of the decade" (p. 8).

The critic prophesizes the destruction of the theater

and adds a sinister prediction. As the rope bears the weight of the man who hanged himself, such is also the success of the play; the full houses that it plays to would not save the Moscow Art Theater from death.

Reading the reviews from those years one is struck by their extraordinary crudeness. Even the astute and erudite Lunacharsky could not keep from kicking Bulgakov, and wrote that the atmosphere in the play *The Days of the Turbins* is like that of a dog's wedding. (*Izvestiya*, Oct. 8, 1926). M.A. reacted wisely and with restraint (for the time being) in the face of all these attacks.

Zoya's Apartment is also playing to full houses. In commemoration of the successes at the theater we named our cat Muka's firstborn "Sold-Out."

> *To stoke the stove, that is my task.*
> *Upon the same the cats do bask.*
> *Muka is there, Sold-Out is too*
> *She likes it so;*
> *And he does too.*

This excerpt is from the little manuscript book *Muka-Maka* which I mentioned above. Verses by V.D. and drawings by the artist N.A. Ushakov. Our cats inspired not only a poet and an artist but also proved their worth in the epistolary genre. I have saved many family notes addressed to me from the cats. I will quote letter No. 1, retaining the spelling. I must admit that the literary cats did not distinguish themselves for their good grammar.

Dear Mama!
Our dear dad rearranged our cozy apartment. We are very pleased (and I helped Sold-Out, Daddy nearly squashed me when I was crowling under the rug.). Daddy was very sad and did not curse beccos he is nice in spite of he chew on a crunchy fish. But now I sleep deer mama on the ottoman. And me too. Only I am on the chair. mama we would like to be like daddy and we cats beg you that daddy is smart knows everything and not to change. And daddy says to buy. Daddy left and let me out. But we kiss U. now

*you and daddy are on the matress. thats whi i am not.
The Adorred and Loving cats.*

The kitten Sold-Out was given to our good friends the Stronskys. He grew up with them, became prettier and unexpectedly gave birth to kittens for which reason he was demoted from Sold-Out to Zyunka.

On the cover of the little book *Muka-Maka* is a picture of M.A. in a trance; the cats keep him from his work. He is composing *The Crimson Island*.

And there is another little portrait of M.A. He is wearing a coat and a hat and is carrying an armload of firewood (we had a wood stove), but is wearing a monocle just the same. It is obvious that the caricature makes fun of this passion of his. Oh, that monocle! It frequently caused resentment, and some people were even inclined to consider it an indication of counter-revolutionary subversion.

At the same time both of us turned up in the illustrations made by the same N.A. Ushakova for Mayakovsky's children's book *The Story of Vlas*. Just look; there we are, Vlas' parents. M.A. grumbled that he did not look very good.

Gaston Leroux' book *The Man Who Returned From Afar* in Movshenson's translation unfortunately either got lost or was destroyed. N.A. Ushakov drew with colored pencils directly onto the printed text which read more or less like this:

"In the mornings the count and countess went out on the balcony of their castle. The countess petted her greyhounds." (The count was M.A. and I was the countess.)

Kolya Lyamin had added witty comments as if by the translator. But how about the scary places?

The bony hand of a ghost squeezing the wick of a lighted candle was drawn with a dark blue pencil.

"Lyubochka and Maka! Don't read this at night!"

This was such funny and talented mischief! To this day I am grieved that the little book was destroyed by somebody's evil hands.

In the book *Muka-Maka* our ornamented tiled stove was depicted; this was my effort. I wanted it to look like old-fashioned tiles. It obviously captivated the typesetter who had once walked by our open door.

"You have it very nice in there, like a cave," he said and asked us to come with him to the store to help him choose wallpaper for his room. I agreed to come. Mikhail Afanasevich only grinned. In the arcade we were shown some wallpaper with attractive patterns and some plain ones of good quality, but my companion became discouraged and was already absorbed in independent contemplation of the samples hanging on the walls. And suddenly his face lit up.

"I have found it," he said beaming. "You don't mind, do you? Since I am a passionate fisherman I like to look at the water painted on this one." And sure enough, long-legged herons were standing in the water. Each one held a frog in its beak.

If only they were eating fish, but those are frogs, I objected feebly.

That does not matter—it is water, after all...

M.A. teased me later: "No contact between the intelligentsia and the working classes was established; they disagreed on the esthetic platform" he joked.

I do not remember any writers living near us on Levshinsky Street other than Valentin Kataev who came once to get a kitten. He did not come again either to Levshinsky or to Bolshoi Pirogovsky. He and M.A. were friends once, but life led them in different directions. I remember the small, elegant and sturdy theater director Leonid Baratov who used to visit us during that period and the actor from the Korsh Theater, Blyumenthal-Tamarin, a great chatterbox and raconteur—these features are, by the way, characteristic of almost all actors...

The two Ginzburg sisters also belonged to the regular membership of our group. One blonde and one dark, one older and one younger, Roza and Zinaida. The older one, a surgeon, was a beautiful woman; but she did not have that biblical beauty which might be assumed from her last name. On the contrary, she was rather snub-nosed and had red hair that was ever so slightly wavy... They came from Paris. I remember how elegantly dressed she was at one of the evening parties, with strings of pearls around her neck, in the fashion of the time. All our men without exception paid court to her. And in return she smiled affably at each one without exception.

Both sisters were very gregarious. They kept up with

literature and took an interest in the theater. We often went to their comfortable house on Nesvizhsky Lane. One time Roza said that her friend the surgeon, whom she affectionately called "Little Mouse," had told her that a landlord who was a relative of his had an apartment with three small rooms to rent. M.A. jumped at this idea, rode to Bolshoi Pirogovsky and came to an agreement with the landlord, or rather with his wife, who took care of all business. And then we had to move.

The final stage of our life together was beginning: we built our last nest...

Bulgakov skiing with Mkhat actors. Bulgakov and Lyubov are in the back row, second and third from the left.

1926. Left to right: S. Topleninov, M. A. Bulgakov, N. Lyamin, Bulgakova.

OUR LAST NEST

In the old days they would drive from the Kremlin along the straight street along Devichy Field to the Novodevichy Convent in heavy and lumbering royal carriages in the summer and in painted carts in the winter.

If one steps outside our building and looks up to the left one can see the elegant six-storey-high belltower and the outline of the convent. It is an unusually beautiful place. Perhaps one of the best in Moscow.*

Our house (now No. 35 A, Bolshoi Pirogovsky) was formerly the residence of the merchants Reshetnikov but had now been rented to the architect Stuy so that it could be set in order. The former owners' living quarters were on the top floor. Rasputin's chapel used to be there, but now the builder-architect and his wife live there.

To reach our first floor one must go down two steps. On the other hand one must go up two steps from the dining room to reach M.A.'s study through an oak door. It is a very beautifully carved door of dark oak. The doorhandle is a bird's foot made of bronze; the claws grasp a ball... A little landing was formed in front of the entrance to the study. We loved this unique elevated place. Sometimes it served as a proscenium when we played charades, sometimes we just sat on the steps as on a bench.

When we moved in the study was still small. Later on the neighbor left, and we knocked out the wall and enlarged M.A.'s room by eight meters plus a dark closet for trunks, suitcases, and skis.

My room was small and narrow: a bed and beside it a small table, in the corner a dressing table with a chair in front of it. That is all. We were true to our tastes. Maka's study was dark blue. The dining room was yellow. My room was white. The kitchen was small, the bathroom larger.

We brought with us the day bed, the desk—M.A.'s true companion on which he wrote almost all his works—and a few chairs. The two exotic armchairs that I mentioned earlier were given away. The rest of the furniture which had temporarily

---

*The author still lives in this building. (Trans. note)

graced our home was returned to its rightful owner Seryozha Topleninov. All we had left was the oil painting he gave us, signed "Sofronova, 1917." This still life is executed in dark Rembrandt colors, but it is highly revolutionary in its content: in the place of honor, in a silver bowl, lies a potato; in the foreground on a piece of velvet there is an onion; a turnip is lying next to some apples. Good friends located some furniture. On Prechistenka there lived a half-crazy old woman whose relatives were far away and had left her in charge of a large apartment full of furniture, but people started to put pressure on the old woman until she moved into a room under the stairs. She had to get rid of the furniture no matter how. So, we bought six beautiful chairs covered with cornflower blue rep and an extension table. The rest—dressing table, side board, bed—we acquired gradually, for the most part from second-hand shops, and it was only the sofa-bed that we bought from friends (we called it "the flourish"). Lena Ponsova got me the antique floor lamp. I still have all this furniture and to this day its timeless elegance still pleases the eye.

Nadezhda, Maka's sister, who was our constant helping hand, sent us a maid. Marusya was a sweet-looking purely Russian woman with light brown hair and blue eyes. She stayed with us, living there several years until she got married. She was both neat and kind. She did not torment the cats, and when we got a dog, she liked him too. This is how we got the dog. One day when the work on the play *Moliere* was in full swing, I went to the neighborhood store and saw a man holding a shaggy puppy with big eyes. The puppy laid his paws trustingly on his shoulders and looked attentively at the shoppers. I asked the man what he was going to do with the doggie. He answered: "What can I do? I am taking him to the clinic" (that is, to the Department of Vivisection for experiments). I asked him to wait a minute and flew home like a whirlwind. I gave Maka a confused description of the whole situation.

"Let's take him, let's take the puppy, Maka dear, please!"

That is how we got the dog which we called Bouton in honor of Moliere's servant. He soon conquered our hearts, became the general favorite and took part in the charades. In time he made himself so at home in our lives that he became a member of the family. I even hung up another card under Maka's card by the main door; it said: "Bouton Bulgakov. Ring twice." This confused the revenue inspector who came to see us. He asked M.A.: "Are you living with your brother?" After that Bouton's visiting card was removed.

I will return to Marusya. She felt right at home and became one of us. Her specialties were Easter cakes, pies and pancakes. M.A. particularly loved Marusya's Easter cakes. When we had company she was called into the dining room, people clinked glasses with her and drank her health. She would get confused, blush and become very pretty. She was not remarkably witty, but she was observant and resourceful when it came to nicknames. The ski instructor, who went on skiing excursions with a group from the Art Theater, and who selected our house for his visits, was nicknamed "the Pilgrim" by Marusya. This was very a propos. In a hat with unfastened earflaps, carrying the eternal rucksack on his back, with his skis or some sort of sawed-off bits of skis in his hands and always in a hurry, he fully justified his nickname.

As I read through M.A.'s works, I can see that in many cases domestic servants are given roles as members of the family. In *The White Guard* there is Anyuta who grew up in the Turbins' home. In *The Heart of a Dog* the maid Zina and the cook Darya Petrovna are so much "registered," as we say now, in Professor Preobrazhensky's way of life that a home-life without them is not even conceivable.

In the play *Adam and Eve* there is Anya.

In *The Master and Margarita* there is Natasha, half friend, half confidante to Margarita; she makes the night flight with her.

"We too want to live, want to fly," she says...

M.A. or I never returned from a trip without bringing our Marusya some present. Once she asked, "Lyubov Evgenievna, what sort of person is Ryabushinsky?"*

I must confess that I was very surprised, but I explained and was of course interested to know why she wanted to know.

"Well, I met Ageich (Ageich was a locksmith, plumber, jack of all trades and of course a drunkard). And he said to me: 'Marry me, Marusya.'

"'I don't mind if I do,' I said, 'Only you'll have to fix me up

---

*The Ryabushinskys were a wealthy family of bankers and manufacturers.

with all new things and don't expect me to go to work any more.'

'Well, in that case you need to marry Ryabushinsky,' answered Ageich..."

Now I understood the whole thing. She married Ageich just the same. Many times later she came running to me for consolation. A few times the drunk Ageich burst in on us too. The alcohol inclined him toward the divine. In his drunken state he remembered that he used to sing in a church choir when he was young, and he would start to sing hymns. When this happened it was very difficult to send him packing.

"Oh, Goddess, just listen..." He would start his singing.

We were comfortably settled. In the windows we hung up old so-called "Turkish" shawls of wool. The hateful wardrobe naturally stands in the dining room, which is also the living room. The wardrobe was as ugly as it was useful but it did not fit in anywhere. Besides being of direct use to us, it was also used by the cat Muka; whe she had one kitten left, we put a basket on top of the wardrobe and the cat would fly up to her offspring with one leap. This home of hers is called "Solovki."

M.A. never took the cat Muka in his arms; he was too squeamish, but he let her come up on his desk and put a piece of paper under her. He made an exception when she was pregnant; the cat would come up to him, and he would pet her.

The study was M.A.'s realm. The desk (his constant "comrade at arms" for eight and a half years) is turned with the short end to the window. Behind it on the wall there are book shelves painted dark brown. And books: the collected works of the Russian classics—Pushkin, Lermontov, Nekrasov, the adored Gogol, Leo Tolstoi, Alexei K. Tolstoi, Dostoevsky, Saltykov-Shchedrin, Turgenev, Leskov, Goncharov, and Chekhov. There were naturally other Russian writers as well, but I simply cannot remember them all. Two encyclopedias, the Brockhaus-Efron and the *Large Soviet Encyclopedia* edited by O. Yu. Schmidt. The first volume appeared in 1926, but the eighth one, in which M.A.'s works are written about so negligently and his biography is treated so untruthfully, came out in 1927.

Books were his weakness. On one of the shelves there is a notice: "Kindly do not take any books."

Moliere, Anatole France, Zola, Stendhal, Goethe, Schiller...

Several runs of *The Historical Herald* of various dates. On the bottom shelf are magazines, newspaper clippings, scrapbooks with numerous abusive reviews, and the Bible. On the table are candelabra—a gift from the Lyamins—a bronze bust of Suvorov, a picture of me, and mother's cherished little red box that used to contain Coty perfume and on which M.A. had written, "The war of 191..." and than an ink spot. I still have the box.

The lamp is made from a very beautiful dark blue Popov vase, but it is a cripple. Bouton pulled on the cord, knocked it down, and broke it. I was very distressed but M.A. glued it together exactly right, and it served for many years.

I cannot help remembering how Bulgakov celebrates the lampshade, a symbol of warmth, coziness and family in *The White Guard*.

"And then... then it looks awful in the room as in any room where things are stacked up chaotically, and even worse when the lampshade is pulled off the lamp. Never... never take the shade off the lamp! The lampshade is sacred. Never run away like a mouse from danger into the unknown. Doze, read by the lampshade, let the blizzard blow, wait until they come for you."

One of the first visitors to our new home was the radiant young man Roman Karmen whose mother we got to know at Koktebel. He had just started his creative career. As far as I can remember, he photographed M.A., but gave me the picture of some beautiful sheep-dog. That photo is in my possession intact to this day. During the war I was asked by the VOKS,* where I was working temporarily, to go by Karmen's house and pick up some material. Alas! Not a trace was left of the radiance; it was as if he had changed down to the last cell. Roman Karmen was still handsome, but in a stern way. I missed that charming person whose smile used to exude light. Strictly speaking it is completely normal that a man changes as the years go by. It apparently depends on the degree of change...

That winter M. A. bought me a coat of polecat fur. He himself took me to Stoleshnikov Lane and waited while I tried coats on. It was something to see how happy he was over this fur coat, which was immediately nicknamed "the leopard."

---

*All-Union Society for Cultural Relations With Foreign Countries. (Trans. note.)

The leopard served me long and faithfully. Maka obtained no less happiness from another purchase: a golden cigarette case which was not fated to serve long and faithfully. When we were deprived of "fire and water," as M.A. put it, it became necessary to sell the cigarette case.

The year 1927. Our great friend Elena Lansberg once took us to her friends Olga Fedorovna and Valentin Smyshlaev (he was an actor at the 2nd Moscow Art Theater).

It was noisy. There were many people present. More and more actors from that theater. The center of attention was an attractive girl who looked Armenian and had abundant blond hair. Everybody kept asking her, "Hey, Marina, again, again! Macrame costs forty kopeks."

We did not understand the meaning of these words until we heard the monologue of the seamstress from Sudak as it was performed by Marina Spendiarova with an inimitable sense of humor and speaking with a Crimean accent, including all the peculiarities permissible only to those who have lived in the South all of their lives... Later on Marina Spendiarova became our dear friend and our English teacher.

The daughter of the composer Alexander Spendiarov (1871-1928) possessed outstanding creative talents. She sang, drew and was artistically gifted in other ways. Without suspecting it herself, she was also a talented teacher. Both M.A. and I made progress. He made our teacher laugh when he tried to translate into English such untranslatable expressions as "a coffin with music."* Marina laughed and said: "No, no you cannot do that..."

He liked the English word "spoon."

I love to sleep, said M.A., that means I am a "sleeper." (*Spun* in Russian—tr.)

Marina still remembers today how dramatically he came out of the door to his study, stopped on the "proscenium," that is on the landing formed by the steps, and greeted her after a pause.

During that same winter we got to know the composer Alexander Spendiarov. I will quote an extract from his daughter Marina's diary: "Dad and I were at the Bulgakovs'. Lyubov

---

*The Russian expression means approximately: All's well that ends well. (Trans. note)

had asked me ahead of time what Dad's favorite dish was. I said: 'Grouse with red cabbage.' I started looking for Dad in the morning in order to tell him the Bulgakovs' address. I remember his voice on the telephone: 'Is that you Marishka? Well, what is it? So tell me the address... good, I will come, my child.' When I arrived M.A., Lyubov and Daddy were sitting at the table. Dad was sitting with his back to the lights on the Christmas tree. It struck me that he looked so sad, so wilted. He was absorbed in himself, in his gloomy thoughts; he could not get away from his little world, one which at that time was so gloomy, and as he stared into his plate he was telling them about all the troubles that were piling up. After that, somewhat unexpectedly for all of us, came a eulogy to Armenia. It seemed as if he were homesick for Armenia in the turmoil of Moscow."

I liked Alexander Spendiarov, but he turned out to be unusually preoccupied and therefore somewhat absent-minded. The second time that I saw the composer, he was on the composer's podium, and, naturally he appeared to be a completely different man.

Summer. It is hot. We were getting ready to go to the Spendiarovs' cottage at Sudak on the Crimean coast, a two-storey, friendly-looking house right on the seashore; it is possible to throw on a robe and run down to swim. Our room was darkish and cool.

There were many people—the large Spendiarov family: the mother (not the father); four daughters, Tatyana, Elena, Marina and Maria; two sons, Tasya and Lyosya. The two Lyamins arrived here too. M.A. went back to Moscow after staying only a short time, but promised to come back for me. During his absence the Lyamins and I had time to climb Mount Sokol, which we almost fell off of, to go to Alchak, to the Genoese fortress, to Novy Svet... M.A. suddenly turned up, saying he had hired a motor boat which would take us straight to Yalta.

We rode in the boat for a long time. Two fishermen drove the boat, one old and one young, both deeply sun-tanned. The sea sparkled so beautifully in the sun; the water was calm and quite near, not far away over the railing of the steamer, but near—all you had to do was stretch out your hand to reach the silver and gold brocade. M.A. was contented; he suggested that we put in every time he saw some little cove on the shore. When we arrived at Yalta I was a little dizzy, and things were swimming before my eyes. We stopped over with some friends of M.A.'s the Tikhomirskys (memory, are you bringing back the correct name of these kind and hospitable people?)

The following day we went to Autka to see Anton Chekhov's villa and the commemorative museum. We went up and up. The house is beautifully situated on the cliff. Maria, the writer's sister received us affectionately and took us around the rooms. The house appeared elegant and even luxurious, but at the same time comfortable. At that time Chekhov's brother Mikhail, the writer's first biographer, was still living there. We especially liked Chekov's study. A semicircle of stained glass around the large Italian window softened the rays of the Crimean sun, and the room seemed cool. A landscape by Levitan hung over the brick fireplace straight across from the desk. Everything on the table was the way it was when Chekhov himself was there. There were many photographs on the walls. They lent a shade of special intimacy to the whole room. M.A. had been here before. I asked him: "Maka, would you like to have a study like this?" He did not say anything, but nodded in agreement. At this desk Chekhov wrote many fine things: the stories "The Lady With a Dog," "The Bishop," "Christmas," "The Betrothed," "In the Ravine" and two plays, *The Three Sisters* and *The Cherry Orchard*. If he had not been sick and died so young, how much more joy might not mankind have received! Maria was smiling happily. Mikhail was displeased with something.

Bulgakov loved Chekhov, but not with that fanatic love so typical of certain Chekhov specialists; he loved him affectionately, as one loves a good and clever older brother. He was especially enthusiastic over his notebooks. Sometimes he quite unexpectedly quoted from them—"my Lutheran wife, when you sleep you say 'chi-pwa, chi-pwa...''

We used to play this game. We asked each other any sort of question, and the other had to answer at once without thinking it over and without making a choice. Once he asked me, "Which work of literature do you think is the most well-written?"

I replied: "Lermontov's 'Taman.'" He said, "That's what Anton Pavlovich thinks too." And then he cited the letter in which Chekhov said so. Now that I think back I can see that he actually knew quite a lot. His memory was also excellent.

I was very pleased when Maria Chekhov came to see us on Pirogovsky. There was something unusually simple and attractive about her.

The year 1928. April. An uncertain Moscow spring. One could not even tell whether the buds on the trees were swelling or not. And suddenly M.A. became eager to go south, first to Tiflis, then via Batum to Cape Green. We left in the afternoon of April 21 in an International Sleeping Car, in which Maka claims to relax particularly well.

The forests around Moscow flashed by and the dismal central Russian plains flew by. It got warmer. Our car was almost empty; it was not high season yet. The poet Nikolai Aseev was on the same train. The Kamerny Theater actress Nazarova, a blond and rosy child-woman, occupied one compartment together with a soldier. He was wearing riding breeches and boots, but had a pyjama shirt on, and his Nagan revolver hung down clumsily and unattractively from below the pyjama shirt. Passengers usually get acquainted quickly and have long and sometimes interesting conversations because they have nothing else to do, but we were all quiet. Aseev exchanged greetings with Bulgakov from afar. After a little more than three days and nights he had exchanged altogether a couple of sentences with me...

What a delightful transition from the snowy fields to sun, green grass, and tulips. I no longer remember the reason why, but we stopped in the middle of a field... Everybody poured out of the cars looking anxiously at the train, wondering if it would let us down. But then, intoxicated with the spring air, we returned to our seats.

April 24, in Tiflis. We were met at the station by Olga Turkul, a small blond and modest woman whom M.A. already knew from his days in Vladikavkaz. She gave us lodging for the first night. The following day we moved to the Orient Hotel on Rustaveli Boulevard. Late in the evening the city was very beautiful and mysterious. The dark outlines of the mountains are faintly visible, and the streetlights seem different somehow, like spangles on black velvet.

It was hot. We slept with our windows open. I walked

around coatless, which is not customary there until the first of May. That is what O.K. Turkul explained to me. M.A. was supposed to conduct negotiations with the Russian Dramatic Theater about a possible production of *Zoya's Apartment.*

The meeting with the theater director took place. I remember what he looked like and the face of his wife, an actress who played leading roles. Some actors from the theater came and joined the two of them and us, making up a party of eight, and we set out for the basement restaurant with the alluring name "Sympathy." The dim golden walls were decorated with portraits: Pushkin, Lermontov, Gorrky (that is how it was spelled), all of them in medallions made of grape clusters and all looking alike with the same typically Georgian face. Behind a bar set with national hors d'oeuvres made with tarragon, coriander, pepper (onion puree), and watercress, stood another man with a black moustache just like Pushkin, Lermontov and Gorky.

The dinner party lasted five hours. The toasts were continuous. All you could hear was "Alaverde to you, alaverde to you!* There came a moment when a quarrel suddenly broke out at the table next to us. Two people jumped up, emitting guttural shouts; they threw their coats on the edge of the small pool where the beloved Georgian fish were swimming, and I closed my eyes so that I would not see the knife fight—but when I opened them the two were sitting at the table peacefully clinking their glasses of their favorite Kahetian wine...

We went swimming in the sun. We swam at the sulphur baths. We walked down the Veritsky Hill to the old town and across the river Kurul. But the Kurul is swift and yellow. It is not the least bit inviting to swim there. First the hanging balcony, then the stone steps of the steep flight of stairs leading up the hill suddenly reminded me vividly of Constantinople.

Our stay in Tiflis was almost clouded by a certain event. One evening O.K. Turkul came by to take us to the movies. M.A. declined, saying that he was going to lie down and rest for a while he always slept after dinner, although with his sweet and winning smile, he insisted that he was not sleeping but only thinking of his new work). I went to the movies and took the room key with me after I had locked up Maka, who was getting ready

---

*Turkish: *Allah verdi*, means "God gave." (Trans. note)

to go to bed. O.K. and I were delayed by something and when we got to the "Orient" I understood that something had happened. The cab drivers with two-horse carriages standing in a line in front of the hotel were shouting merrily at each other and looking at one of the windows. M.A. was sticking his tousled head out of the window, and when he saw me he shouted to the entire Rustaveli Boulevard,

"I did not expect this of you Lyubasha!"

Downstairs in the lobby the Georgian hall porter rushed up to me,

"Vay you go away? Vay you take away key? He be so angry, so angry. He need key, he stomp feet."

"But do you not really have another key?"

"Vee have not another."

I ran upstairs and begged forgiveness for my "sin."

The same O.K. took us to a pastry shop on a side street where she introduced us to the owner, a Frenchwoman, and also to her niece Marika Chimishkian, half-French, half-Armenian, a young and very pretty girl who later became connected with our family for many years. To her, in her capacity as a nurse and friend, fell the sad lot of watching at the bed-side of the dying writer Bulgakov.

We wanted to look around the city. M.A. rented a car, and we drove about to our hearts' content; and in the evening we went to the theater to see *The Inspector General* with Stepan Kuznetsov. Not far from us, in a box, sat an old Georgian lady dressed in the national costume, a low cap pulled up in front and braids hanging down the sides of the face. A transparent white veil was fastened to the back of the cap. Everybody in Tiflis knew this woman—she was Stalin's mother.

I saw the first act and got bored.

"Listen, folks," I said to Maka and Marika. "It is pretty boring to see this kind of *Inspector* after seeing Meyerhold's. You can stay here but I'm going out to wander around for a while," (I love to walk around unknown streets).

This is a good time to recall that in 1926 Meyerhold had put on *The Inspector General*. M.A. and I went to the dress rehearsal, and when we returned home in a cab we quarrelled so much that the frightened driver kept turning around to look. I enjoyed the performance; it was interesting. I said that a director has the right to show the period by other means than the furniture, especially if he has the talent to do it; but M.A. believed that such arbitrary liberties with the play distorted the author's idea and bore witness to the director's lack of respect for him. I think that we probably screamed out our quarrel over all of Moscow...

It was already the beginning of May. We travelled to Cape Green via Batum.

I did not like Batum. It rained, and the city looked gray and ugly in the rain. I wrote at length about this in a letter to the Lyamins, but my "censor" M.A. crossed out all of it.

It is amazing to what an extent he loved the Caucasian coast—Batum, Makhindzhauri, Tsikhidziri, but especially Cape Green, although to judge from *Notes on the Cuff* he did not experience great happiness on his travels there. "My tears are as salty as the sea water," he wrote.

He also refers to Cape Green in the play *Adam and Eve*. The hero and heroine dream of shaking off all city worries and going to Cape Green for a month and a half on their honeymoon.

Here we put up at a pension run by the Dane Stor in what used to be the villa of the Baryatinsky princes. To reach it you had to survive a climb of a hundred steps. We arrived when the camelias had finished blooming, and the sandy path was strewn with these royal flowers. I was especially impressed with the abundance of the flowers. "We are finally where it is warm," I wrote to the Lyamins. "Yesterday I saw the famous green ray. But that is not the main thing. The flowers are. Goodness how many there are!" At the end of the letter Maka added, "Dear Tata and Kolya! Tell everyone hello. I often think of you. Your Maka."

When they made the film *The Lame Gentleman* from the novel by Alexei Tolstoi they needed Nice. It would be difficult to imagine a better Nice than this little place.

They gave us a large room with three enormous windows, as if in a church. Swallows flew in through one, across the room and out through another. Spaciousness was evident everywhere in the way the rooms, the terraces, and the hallways were laid out. On the bottom floor were the Stors' hall and living quarters. Their family consisted of the jovial and simple Danish landlord, who said "shockel" for jackal, his beautiful and sour Russian wife, and their twelve-year old daughter Svetlana, who was the very image of her father.

It was hot and humid. It smelled of eucalyptus. The oleander groves were blooming where I went for walks with Svetlana until one day when the worried M.A. came to meet us and said,

"You are going to catch it, Lyubasha."

And indeed Mme. Stor looked coldly at me and asked me drily not to take her daughter on long walks any more, since the Kurds were migrating and they might steal Svetlana.

M.A. did not especially care to set out on long walks, but almost the day after we arrived we went to the local Botanical Garden and we were very pleased when a nice red dog joined us. He was not homeless at all, but simply seemed to love company. He took us to the gate of the Botanical Garden. He came in with us, walked ahead looking back now and then and waited for us if necessary. We composed a couplet: "Man gladly speeds/Where his dog leads." After looking around the garden the three of us left through another gate.

The wide halls in our villa were badly lit, and since I had been reading the adventures of the vampire Count Dracula I was afraid to walk to one remote corner in the hall and begged M.A. to stand guard and to sing or whistle while he did. I remember how he sang "Lovely eyes, eyes like the sea, the azure color of the blue sky" and kept saying, "Lord, how stupid!" and continued singing. "Sometimes you laugh, sometimes you grieve."

This was funny, of course, but Count Dracula required a victim...

If you look at a photograph of M.A. taken at Cape Green, it becomes clear at once that he was calm and happy then.

After Cape Green we went on the Georgian Military Highway to Vladikavkaz. Our car was the first one that had got through the pass. Nothing terrible happened; we put on chains and shoveled snow once. In Vladikavkaz some representatives from the authorities received us as the first swallows, and little boys shouted, "Hurrah!"

Our train to Moscow left at two o'clock in the morning. We walked around town. M.A. did not think that it had changed much during the six or seven years which had gone by since he lived there.

Bulgakov in the Caucasus, April 25, 1927.

I remember that the lilac was blooming and that there was a lot of it. In order to kill time we bought tickets to a midget theater. They were performing the operetta *Les Bayadère*. The theater was full to overflowing. I have never seen such a funny spectacle—it was as if children were playing at being grown-ups. The hero-lover was especially captivating. He was wearing a cork helmet, flapped his arms and tried to express passion with his voice. The applause was thunderous. He was drowned in lilacs.

Later on at home in Moscow Maka imitated the midget actor; he assumed a comical stony expression and walked without bending his knees, and he also moved his head a special way.

I have a foreboding that the last summarizing chapter is going to be confused. I can remember many things, both bad and good. There is some of everything here—the most different kinds of people, the most diverse plays—*Flight, Molière* (it was dedicated to me), *Adam and Eve* and the story "The Consultant with a Hoof" which was the basis for the novel *The Master and Margarita*. (I will return a bit later to the works of those years.)

In 1929 or 1930 M.A. and I once went to visit his old acquaintances, the Moiseenkos (they lived in Nirenzee House on Gnezdnikovsky Lane). An interesting lady with nicely styled hair was sitting at the table—Elena Nyurenberg whose married name was Shilovskaya. She soon became my friend and began to visit us at home often and without ceremony.

That is how this woman who later became M.A. Bulgakov's third wife entered the orbit of our family.

Our regular visitors were still Kolya and Tata Lyamin, Anna Tolstaya and her husband P.S. Popov, Seryozha Topleninov, the Nikitinskys, Petya Vasilev, the Ponsov sisters (Elena had already become the wife of the actor Viktor Stanitsyn; Lidya was married to the literary critic Andrei Saburov).

My aunt came visiting from Sevastopol. M.A. nicknamed her "The Iron Woman," and here is why. We took her to see *The Days of the Turbins*. She asked to go, noting that it would be awkward to return to Sevastopol from Moscow without having seen this sensational play. During the performance she did not smile a single time. And to think that this was my mother's sister! My mother would have cried and smiled through her tears many times.

The Iron Woman gave me a green living-room suite called "Sablinsky," which the peasants had divided up among their huts after the Revolution. M.A. became very cheerful, and said that she would not have made us happier even if she had given us the Moscow Kremlin.

Soon after that, my aunt's husband's nephew, Valery Vilgelmov, came to stay with us. I was in no way related to him, but he claimed to be my first cousin. He was noted for answering all questions without a moment's hesitation. Maka played a trick on him.

"It would be interesting to know how much an adult lion eats," he suddenly asked, and quick as lightening the "cousin" mentioned a fantastic figure. Poor "Know-it-all!" He died in the first months of the war in the People's Home Guard. It was quite incomprehensible how he was accepted there; he had a bad back and always wore and orthopedic corset.

Literary girls came too. Usually they hardly even said hello to me, since they regarded me as an obstacle to their possible happiness. I can remember two of them. One had black eyebrows set far apart and looked like an Old Believer's madonna. She read a story about a puppy entitled "Splash." The other one looked like Don Basilio from *The Marriage of Figaro*, but what she read I do not remember. M.A. was very indulgent with them. Beginning writers came too. One of them was not without talent but was very ill mentally; he could never get rid of his auditory hallucinations. Several times M.A., Kolya Lyamin and I went out with groups of students, and we spent the time very pleasantly discussing various literary problems.

As M.A.'s popularity as a writer grew, women paid more attention to him. Many of them (Nomina sunt odiosa) showed an extremely high degree of persistence...

First I will recollect our happy life. It is more pleasant that way, more fun to write, and it seems that the black days recede and go far away somewhere. It so happened in 1928 that the three plays *The Days of the Turbins, Zoya's Apartment* and *The Crimson Island* were playing at the same time. But fellow writers and fellow journalists were vigilant. The time would come (and that time was no longer distant) when there would be nothing. And in the meantime—in the meantime various people came to see us. Of the writers I remember Ilf and Evgeny Petrov, Nikolai Erdman, Olesha and Zamyatin, and of the actors M.M. Yanshin, N.P. Khmelev, and I.M. Kudryavtsev, and V. Ya. Stanitsyn. Sometimes the small and sharp Savonarola-like profile of the artist N. E. Radlow appeared, when he came from Leningrad.

After Khmelev had played the role of Alexei Turbin I really wanted to meet him. A disappointment was in store for me. People like him, one says are "neither fish nor fowl." So how can one explain the secret of the way he was transformed when acting? All his roles were great events. Especially Dostoevsky's *Uncle's Dream*. This was the acme of the actor's art. M.A. wanted to test for Mozglyakov's role in the same play. He performed a little for me, unintentionally imitating Vladimir Sinitsyn.

The actress and director M.I. Knebel devoted some interesting pages to Khmelev in her book *My Whole Life*. She makes a complicated psychological analysis of his personality, emphasizing his immaturity, naivete, and suspiciousness as well as his anxiety, which was sometimes a burden to those around him. She writes: "Khmelev's intuition was phenomenal; it was a pleasure to study the development of the creative process in him, because of all the unexpected discoveries hidden in this process" (p. 442). He could feel the entirety of the character with a sixth sense, according to the director A.D. Popov—apropos of Khmelev's interpretation of Ivan the Terrible in A.N. Tolstoi's play *The Difficult Years*.

When I write about the play *Flight*, in which the main role, the most responsible and complicated role, was intended for Khmelev, I will return to him...

While the good days still lasted, one dream never left me. I was not attracted by jewellery or by clothes. I wanted to have a small car. Our poet V.D. wrote some verses with this refrain:

> *Oh, hardly, hardly does the money*
> *Suffice to buy a little car...*

When our old chums came to visit us—the Ponsovs, Seryozha Topleninov and Petya Vasilev—we organized "flea battles." M.A. was passionately fond of this childish game and was extraordinarily successful at it. For this reason he received the nickname "Maka-Bulgaka, King of the Fleas." The Kamerny Theater actor T.F. Voloshin and his diminutive and sweet Japanese Wive Iname-san (Chrysanthemum) came to do flea fighting. Sometimes we went to a stadium to play tennis. Both of them, the poor dears, perished in 1937, and what happened to their little son, Emio-san (Sun-ray) I do not know.

During those years we often went to the "Circle" the club for art workers on Staropimenovsky Lane. Almost every time Demian Bedny, a very solid-looking and sturdily built man, was seated at a particular table. I would never have guessed that he was a poet. I would sooner have imagined that he was a military man with a general's rank.

Bulgakov and Mayakovsky often did battle in the billiard room, and as I sat there watching them, I was thinking how different they were. To begin with, M. A. preferred to play "pyramid," a rather subtle game, while Mayakovsky leaned towards "American" and became a great master at that game.

I was not only thinking of how different they were, but I also wondered why M.A. played with such a stony and reserved look on his face. The relationship between Bulgakov and Mayakovsky has never been dealt with in print but it is necessary to discuss it. What is the meaning of the following speech delivered by Mayakovsky and reported by A.V. Lunacharsky in *Theaterical Politics of the Soviet Government* (Leningrad, Oct. 2, 1926). It is not pleasant to quote from that address, but from my point of view it is necessary.

Is there anything that Anatoly Vasilievich was not totally and one hundred percent correct about. What if he thought that this same The White Guard *was only an accident in the repertory of the Art Theater. I think that is a correct logical conclusion. They began with Aunt Manya and* Uncle Vanya *and ended up with* The White Guard *(laughter.) It would be a hundred times nicer, in my opinion, that this should be picked on and torn to pieces than to be concealed beneath the banner of apolitical art. Take the notorious book by Stanislavsky* My Life in Art, *that celebrated epicurean book; it is the same old* The White Guard—*and there you will see how they sing the praises of the merchant class right in the introduction. And in this respect* The White Gurad *signed their calling-card, and was just the last step in the Art Theater's road from apoliticism to* The White Guard...

In respect to the policy of banning plays, I believe that this policy is totally harmful... To ban a play which exists, which only concentrates and brings to light certain moods which exist—such a play ought not to be banned. And if two Komsomol members are taken out of the theater, then, come on, I can guarantee the failure of that play—they won't kick me out. Two hundred men will whistle, and we will not fear the wreckage, scandal, police and proceedings... (applause).

...We happened to give Bulgakov the possibility (under cover of the bourgeoisie)to squeak—and he squeaked. But we won't let him any more. (Voice from the audience: "You will ban him?") No, not ban him. What do you gain by banning? Only that the banned literature will be taken into corners and read with as much enjoyment as I got from reading a handwritten copy of Esenin's poetry two hundred times.

*Revolutionary writers are getting along badly... we need to promote the new art... (*he speaks out against the pornographic "Relics" by Kalinnikov*).*

So here is this disgraceful policy of permitting all our works to enter the channel of free trade; that which can be bought is bought, it's good, but everything else is bad. This is extremely harmful for the politics of the theater, literature and anything else. And it is definitely more harmful to us than the scabby and ragged White Guard. *(V.V.* Mayakovsky, Polnoe sobranie sochinenii. *Moscow: GIKhL, 1959, XII, 303-305).*

Now we can easily explain that the stony-suffering expression on Bulgakov's face.

Thank goodness that V.A. Lunacharsky did not authorize this action, one worth of a Chinese anarchist.

I have often reread Mayakovsky's speech and am always puzzled. Why is it bad to ban a play and remove it from the repertory, while it is all right, in fact it is good, to bring two hundred people to the theater and create an unprecedented scandal?

Mayakovsky's attacks on Stanislavsky's book were also not very intelligent. Just think how he glorified the merchant class—he thanked them warmly for their help in founding the theater!

When the chorus of biting and hooting grew fuller Mayakovsky did not fail to take a jab at Bulgakov in his poem "Nouveau bourgeois" (1928):

> *For a box*
> *In the window*
> *of the theater box-office*
> *he pokes*
> *a polished fingernail*
> *he*
> *gives*
> *a social order*
> *for* The Days of the Turbins,
> *to the Bulgakovs.*
>
> *Komsomol pravda*, February 29, 1928.

"He," i.e., the *nouveau bourgeois*.

Even allowing for a poetic hyperbole, it's still impossible to understand where in the Soviet Union such bourgeois were to be found and where they were so strong and numerous that they could give a social command for *The Days of the Turbins* — and for whom? And it is so very scornful to put the name in plural—the Bulgakovs.

In 1928 Mayakovsky's play *The Bedbug* was published. One of the characters, Zoya Berezkina, pronounces the word "buza" (disorder, bad business).

"*The Professor*: Comrade Berezkina, you've taken to living in the past. You're talking a language I can't understand— just like a dictionary of obsolete words. What does *buza* (bad business) mean? Business... let's see, Bohemia... bubliki... Bulgakov... bureaucracy... business. Ah, yes!'"

If Mayakovsky had said in the poem "Nouveau Bourgeois" that *The Days of the Turbins* was written for the consumption of NEP-men, then M.A. Bulgakov's death as a writer is predicted in *The Bedbug*. Mayakovsky was a bad prophet. Bulgakov did not end up in the dictionary of dead words but of words that have come to life again and are living and resounding with a new force...

I can remember the regular visitors to the "Circle," the artists from the Maly Theater Prov Sadovsky and Mikhail Lenin. One time we were going to have supper with Vera Sokolova, an actress at the Moscow Art Theater. A middle-aged fellow with black hair came up to us; he looked like a prosperous lawyer and spoke only a few but very expressive words to Vera. He told her that he had admired her acting for a long time, that she had created an unforgettable character in the role of Elizaveta Petrovna and that he would, with her permission, present her with her portrait, or at least a picture that looked like her. He lived quite nearby and would go and get the portrait.

We sat down, very intrigued. Vera was confused and blushed. After a short time the dark-haired man appeared and gave Vera an excellent oval miniature on metal with the head of a woman. Perhaps it is still intact and in the possession of Andrei, the son of V.S. Sokolova and L.V. Baratov. How elegantly and unobtrusively this Max Benediktov, an antiquarian, made his worship of Sokolova's talent known; she was indeed a sensitive artist.

During this winter (1928) we went skiing with people from the Art Theater. Our instructor Vladimir, the one whom our Marusya nicknamed "the pilgrim," led us to the hills near the village of Gladyshevo and to Sokolniki. The best skier in our group was Ivan Kudryavtsev (Nikolka in *The Turbins*). He was very light, weightless, like "an angel among the clouds" as M.A. put it.

There was a snack bar in Gladyshevo where we halted. A sign decorated the wall: "Unsuitable langwitch is not to be used." And we did not use any. We only annihilated fried eggs and sausages with pleasure, washing them down with beer. As I remember it, Kudryavtsev whispered: "Perhaps it is like this in heaven..." We went down the steep hills, fell head over heels and lost our skis, but our instructor would go down on one ski. Our friend Irina Kislovskaya had come with us. She stands to Stanitsyn's left in the group photo. M. A. very much liked the fact that she would start down from any height without any hesitation. Once she fell head first and was completely buried

Lyubov and her horse.

in the snow, but she shook off the snow and continued downhill as if nothing had happened.

Besides skiing I developed a passion for another sport—horseback riding. I rode with a group at Podvoysky's on Povar Street (now Vorovsky Street). Our chief N.I. Podvoisky sometimes came down to the stables. For a short time I went with Ksenia Karlovna, the wife of the actor Mikhail Chekhov. We shared a horse named Nina, a stubborn and rather stupid creature who often reared up on her hind legs or did a "candle" as it is called by horsemen.

The Chekhovs soon went abroad and Nina was liquidated.

A motorcycle with a sidecar would come for M.A. when he needed it, much to the enjoyment of our Marusya, who now called it "the turtle" and looked affectionately at its owner, a far from ugly young man.

Marika Chimishkian came from Tiflis to stay with us. Marusya heated a bath for her. We had stoves everywhere for heating, and M.A. sometimes laid a fire himself in the stove in his study. Whe he was stoking it, he loved to look at the coals crusted over with gold, but he was always afraid of carbon monoxide. At that time Pavel Markov, the literary critic who worked at MXAT, came to visit us at Pirogovsky. M.A. said to him, "A little old man is visiting us; he tells stories very well. He's taking a bath now, but he'll finish and be out in a few minutes..."

How surprised Markov was when it was Marika who came into the dining room instead of a little old man. I already said that she was very beautiful. Markov started laughing. You had to hear his laugh to appreciate it—it was not exactly a sob or a choke or a squeal. In this respect he was unique. Maka was satisfied. He was happy when his jokes were successful, and they were almost always successful.

I remember one time when we went to see our old friend Elena Lansberg. How the subsequent game started I cannot remember exactly, nor do I know who initiated it. We pretended that I had come alone, and M. A. was supposed to ring on the main door later on and pretend that he was the revenue inspector who had come to register the antiquities in Elena's possession. The performance was for the benefit of her visiting relative from Leningrad... A ring. Into the room came an unpleasant person (he really was). He introduced himself as the revenue inspector for the local district and started to jump from subject to subject, making insidious remarks. The relative (Olechka was her name) was sitting with a sort of frozen expression on her face; then she called Elena into the next room and whispered anxiously.

"He's some sort of imposter. And you didn't even ask to see his identification."

When she returned to the "revenue inspector" she said that this sort of visit was not done in Leningrad...Then we told her the truth. I must say that M.A. carried out his part very well. As a silent spectator, I saw how easily he "entered into the character," changed his way of walking and talking and his gestures...

I remember yet another game. One evening when I was not there Maka got bored. Then he telephoned another friend of ours, Zinaida Dorofeeva and told her with a faltering voice that he was feeling very bad and that he was dying. Zika (that was her name at home) and her friend were finishing a home permanent. Without setting their hair, they wrapped their wet heads in towels and both of them anxiously rushed over to our house on Pirogovsky Street, where a merry host was awaiting them with supper and wine. I finally got there expecting to find him with one foot in the grave as the folk say. I will not hide the fact that I was very surprised to see ladies in turbans there. But while we drank a glass of wine, all was explained to everyone's satisfaction.

After Marika's arrival new acquaintances started to come to see us. She brought her friend Kira Andronikova, the sister of the movie actress Nata Vachnadze. Kira had none of her sister's sweet beauty. The latter's eyes were like stars, her mouth like a rose bud, her cheeks like peaches, the whole arsenal of Eastern feminine allurements. Kira was more like a stately Georgian youth with clear and open facial features. She married the writer Boris Pilnyak and shared his sad fate.

Marika further acquainted us with an entertaining couple He was Tonin Piccin, an Italian who was short and lively and looked like a hairy black bug, hot-tempered and always ready to get angry or to laugh. She was Russian, Tatyana, a very feminine and elegant woman in love with her husband and attached to Russia with all her soul. I can imagine how she grieved when she had to go to Italy with her husband. He was an engineer, a representative of the Fiat company, but all of them were turned out of the Union "because they're not needed." If both of them were alive now they would definitely return to our country, now that Fiat is again in good grace.

M.A. wrote funny "at home" poems to them which I of course do not remember. I only remember two lines having to do with Piccin:

> *I'll break your head, he shrieks*
> *As he demands his keys.*

—the keys to the car which Tatyana Sergeevna drove (and drove quite well). They visited us and we them. Often one of them dropped by with the car to take us for a ride.

A fine spring day in 1929. A large open Fiat stopped in front of our house; it was Monsieur Piccin who had come for us. We came out, Maka, Marika and I. In the car we made the acquaintance of a handsome young man in a straw hat (he was the best looking man that I have ever seen). He was the Italian journalist and publicist Curtio Malaparte,* a man with an uncommonly stormy biography, which one can find out about in all European reference books—although with some discrepancies. This name, or rather pseudonym, was often mentioned in our press. His real name was Kurt Zuckert.

As a tender youth he volunteered for the French front in the First World War. He was gassed—the Germans were using gas then for the first time.

He was responsible for many sharp journalistic pieces: "Living Europe," "Lenin's Mind," "The Volga Starts in Europe," "Kaput" and many other articles which were much talked about abroad but never translated into Russian. To judge only from the titles they display a tendency towards the left. But it was not only that way. At first an admirer of Mussolini, then his bitter enemy, he paid for this with a difficult exile to the Liparian Islands. He died in 1957. A papal nuncio was in attendance at his death-bed—according to foreign sources—

---

*When asked why he chose his pseudonym he said, "Because the name Bonaparte is already taken."

so that he would not refuse the Catholic sacrament at the last moment. But here I am running ahead. In the period I am describing, he was a charming and cheerful man, pleasant to look at and nice to be with. He unfortunately stayed in Moscow for a short time only.

I will move on to some of the most unpleasant pages of my memoirs—to Sergei Ermolinsky. One might get a false impression of his personality from his publications in the press (I have in mind the journal *Theater*, No. 9, 1966, "About Mikhail Bulgakov").

In the summer of 1929 he met our Marika and fell in love with her. One evening he came for her. She collected what little baggage she had. I was sad. Marusya cried as she stood in the window.

Ermolinsky lived with Marika for twenty-seven years, which did not prevent him from referring to her in the abovementioned recollections in passing as a "very sweet girl from Tbilisi." He did not even deign to call her his future wife (and this after all those twenty-seven years of living together).

It is too bad that there is no special test for memoirists to determine the truthfulness and sincerity of their authors. Ermolinsky would fare badly with the lie detector. I will leave aside all his excursions into psychology. There is much that he does not even suspect, even though he pretends to have been the confidant of M.A. Bulgakov, who never felt any particular liking for Ermolinsky, although he was on friendly terms with Marika.

Some notes which are left from those years even bear witness to this. I have an envelope in front of me; M.A. wrote on it: "To Marika Artemievna for Lyubanya" (not his "friend" Sergei, but to Marika).

And here is a later note, from February 5, 1933: "Lyubanya, I stopped by at Marika's at dinner time (5:30) but something had apparently happened there—it was dark in the windows and only the dachshunds were barking. Kisses—M."

Nor are there ever any references to Sergei Ermolinsky in other old papers. When one reads this "opus" in the journal *Theater* which is, unfortunately written quite glibly, one is repeatedly struck by the author's lack of principle. It is not my intention to refute Ermolinsky point by point, including all his insinuations and garbled accounts, but I do have to say a few things. Although his recollections are already overloaded with quotes (Mandelstam, Herzen twice, M. Prishvin, Hemingway, Zabolotsky, P. Vyazemsky, Gogol, Pushkin, Griboedov, P. Mirimsky), I will add one more, from *Woe from Wit*: "There is nothing here but deceit." It *is* deceit. And what deceit! To begin with the author's purpose. Ermolinsky himself occupies the first place; the second place—for what it is worth—is allotted to the dying Bulgakov, and the third place—such as it is—is given to Fadeev, an important figure on the literary horizon.

You see, just like all our guests at Pirogovsky Street, Ermolinsky was met by our chestnut-colored dog Bouton. But it was not the dog Bouton, but I, the mistress of the house, who had been the wife of the writer Bulgakov for eight and a half years. The novel *The White Guard*, the novella *Heart of a Dog* and the play *Molière* were dedicated to me. Ermolinsky could not help knowing this, but in his two-faced way, he forgets what is convenient for him to forget, for instance his twenty-seven years of marriage to Marika Chimishkian. He "forgot" to mention M.A.'s younger sister Elena, who was beside her beloved brother up to his last breath. When arranging situations to his own advantage, Ermolinsky simply brushed aside the living people who were close to M.A.

During one of the last meetings with his sister Nadezhda before he died, M.A. said to her, "If you only knew how I fear the memoir writers."

One can imagine how upset he would get over all the cheap, pretentious writing, the immodesty and the baseness of Ermolinsky's memoirs.

Leisurely and without any hopes that I would acquire an automobile, I nevertheless registered for the first state-organized courses for drivers at the Krasnopresnensky Regional Soviet, but I did not stop going horseback riding at the stables. A funny telephone conversation between M.A. and the drunk instructor at the stables took place during this period.

Stenographic record.

Ring.
I: Hello.
Voice: Are you Lyubov Evgenievna?
I: Sorry she is not here.
Voice: Why not? She is a smart woman. Always when things aren't right...(hiccup) I tell her...
I: What do you tell her...
Voice: Did she go to the stables?
I: No, she went shopping.
Voice: (Sternly) What?
I: Who is speaking?
Voice: Are you her husband?
I: Yes. Please tell me who I'm speaking to?
Voice: Kstin Aplonich (hiccup) Kram (hiccup)
I: Call again at five, she'll be here for dinner.
Voice: (Annoyed) Huh... can't I eat too... But that isn't what I called for. Merci. It's been a pleasure. I h-hope you can come?
I: Merci.
Voice: Come and see me—I'll be here Wednesday? Huh? (hiccups frequently) She shouldn't go riding. She shouldn't. You understand?
I: Hm...
Voice: (threatening) You understand? She shouldn't go riding at the stables. On days off, I understand, we will give her a horse... but not like this! I used to be an officer of the guard, and I am telling you that she shouldn't, it isn't right. Today she rides and tomorrow she will gallop. She shouldn't (secretively). Do you understand?
I: Hm...
Voice: (Severe) What do you think?
I: I have nothing against her riding.
Voice: Is that all?
I: That's all.
Voice: Hm (hiccup) A car? Great. Did she go to the stables?
I: No, to town.
Voice: (Irritated) Which town?
I: Call her later.

Voice: With pleasure. Come and see me, you and Lyubov Evgenievna. Huh? Did she go to the stables?
I: (Irritated) No...
Voice: She gets exhausted! She should never go riding. (loud hiccups) But...
I: Good-bye... (I hang up the receiver).
      Three minutes' pause
        Ring.
I: Hello.
Voice: (Weak, hoarse, as if dying) Lyu... Bovgeninu.
I: She went out.
Voice: To the stables?
I: No, to town.
Voice: Hm. Oh. Excuse me... for... bother... (dies out).
     (I hang up the receiver.)

Real life was of course different, not so much fun. The time came that our "brother writers" had been dreaming about and striving for so hard: all of Bulgakov's plays were banned.

I was the only woman at the drivers' course which I had registered for with our acquaintance Alexander Talanov. At that time, an automobile represented something unrealizable and fantastic.

It was bothersome to go in the evening and change subways twice to get to the course, but time passed during the lessons. Driving practice took place in the spring—this was the best part. M.A. did not fail to tell all his friends, "Once I was walking down the street with my elegant wife, and suddenly I hear from a five-ton truck which was rolling by, 'Here's mud in your eye!' That's the way truck drivers say hello to my wife..." He made up the part about the mud, of course, but it was true that drivers quite often exchanged greetings when they passed each other.

I have kept many different notes and postcards that M.A. sent from various places. It is now 1928. He went south.

  August 8. Konotop.
  Dear Topson (that is one of my numerous nicknames).

I am having a nice trip, and I enjoy seeing the Ukraine. It is only that I am ravenously hungry on this train. I keep alive on tea and scenery. I am alone in my compartment, and I am very pleased to be able to write. Say hello to all at home, including the cats. I hope that there will not be another one by the time I return (sell it into slavery).

  Tish, tish, tish...

  Your M.

I will clarify what Tish, tish, tish is. When one of us was being noisy the other one quieted him down with that sound.

  August 18, '28. Near Kiev.
  Dear Topson,
  I am beginning to believe in my star. The weather got bad.

  Your M.
Tish, tish, tish!
  How homesick one gets for the place where one was born.

  Aug. 19
  I am in Odessa, Hotel Imperial.

  M.

  Oct. 13, '28. Beyond Kharkov.
  Dear Lyuban,
  A premonition woke me up near Belgorod. And justly so. In Belgorod my International Sleeping Car was sent to hell because a bolt on it broke. And I am travelling in another car, not an international one. The whole night was ruined.

  Further on M.A. writes about the declaration that should be submitted to the revenue inspector. And a postscript: "I don't want that they got rid of the car."

  Yours."

This expression has its own history. When he was a small

Bulgakov's drawings. Above, the house spirit "Rogash." Below, a portrait of the dog Bouton.

boy my nephew was unusually capricious, especially about eating. "I don't want to" was the only thing you ever heard. When he was asked, "But what are you fussing about? You already ate it all up!" Then he said, "I don't want to have eaten it up."

I also have drawings. We had a family house spirit, Rogash. He always turned up unexpectedly and showed his horns; he would turn up for no reason, grumbling and getting angry over nothing. Sometimes Rogash repented and hastened to make amends for his guilt. In M.A.'s drawing he is bringing me, Lyubanya, or abbreviated to Banga, a ring with a diamond of five carats. This ring is, of course, purely symbolic. As far as expensive things are concerned, M.A. gave me some beautiful pearl earrings which I sold at a difficult moment in my life. But the name Banga was incorporated into the novel *The Master and Margarita*. It is the name of Pilate's favorite dog.

Marusya with her unusual Easter cakes was no longer with us—she got married. Now we had Nyusha, or Anna Matveevna, a very literate girl, good-natured, rather lazy and very inquisitive. In order to stifle her curiosity M.A. sometimes writes in Latin characters, but in Russian: "I suspect that the cat is not very full. M."

When I am away for a long time, the cats get upset.

A mom like that
forgets her kat.

P.S. Pappi Wet to bed sadd.

And here is a note from the unusually naughty and spirited kitten Flyushka, who seemed to break everything that he could get his paws on. And as a matter of fact, it was Maka and Anna Matveevna who had been doing their best and then slipped me the fragments as a keepsake, with a short message that read something like this: "Deere mama from Fluchkie."

Flyushka and Bouton would invent noisy games and keep romping until they collapsed from exhaustion. Then they lay on the floor like two spread-out towels, but they kept looking sideways at each other. We called these games Saturnalia. I remember asking Marika's friend, the film photographer Wentzel, if he would photograph their complete grace, inventiveness and joyous playfulness. He said it was impossible; there was no suitable lighting in the apartment, and they would not play under a strong lamp.

The mischevious gray kitten Flyushka that I had brought with me from the Arbat (he was stolen from us while he was sitting in the ventilation window breathing fresh air) was the prototype for the merry cat Behemoth, Voland's companion in *The Master and Margarita*.

"I'm not up to anything. I'm not touching anything. I'm fixing the primus stove..." I can see in this Flyushka's habits.

The cats' messages alternate with M.A.'s own.

Dear little cat,
    For the cupboard, for housekeeping, for the dressmaker, for the dentist, for sweets, for wine, for rugs and car—30 rubles. I took out the cat in the fresh air while he held onto my waistcoat and sobbed.
          Loving you.

It is not you, Larion, that I am angry at.
(This is the last sentence from *Days of the Turbins*. Myshlaevsky says it to Lariosik.)

In the beginning of the summer of 1928 I decided to go down the Volga to the city of Volsk to find the graves of my mother and brother, who had died from spotted typhus during the famine in the Volga region. I needed to put up a fence around their graves.

Shortly before my trip Marika Chimishkian stopped over with us on her way from Leningrad to Tiflis. On the day she was leaving, Mayakovsky called to say that he would come by and pick up Marika (they were old friends from Tiflis). He and the movie actress Nata Vachnadze were sitting in a spacious car. The three of us came along too. V.V. payed a great deal of attention to Marika—chocolate, things to drink on the trip, magazines so that she would not get bored. And all of this in a simple and affectionate way. To tell the truth, that was not what I would have expected from him. We were silent on the way home. I asked, "How come no one is talking? It's as if we were coming from a funeral."

Nata and Maka continued to be silent but Vladimir Vladimirovich said, "It really is like a funeral."

He probably liked our Marika a lot.

My trip by steamer from Nizhny to Volsk along the overflowing Volga was beautiful and pleasant. The scent of lily-of-the-valley was carried by the wind from the surrounding forests. It was a light and joyful fragrance.

Fortunately I found an old friend in Volsk and moved from a dirty furnished room at the "South Pole" to her clean and comfortable little house full of flowers. "The town has become ramshackle and shabby, and it cannot even be estimated how many died," I write to Tata Lyamin in Elatma.

I will quote the entire angry telegraphic letter M.A. set to me in Volsk on June 16.

"Sent hundred fifty rubles by wire struggling terribly at telegraph because monstrous address double digit numerations startling. Has house double digit number of first digit house second digit apartment. Most delicious were mysterious words concerning blushing man or woman, blushing house or blushing apartment or neither house nor apartment but simply face which should figure as money address. I throw out this ruthless missive lets still kiss acknowledge receipt money and sent anykind sensible address Maka."

The second telegram sent from Moscow two days later was more kind.

"House spirits also miss you happy searches successful penates kiss."

"Penates" meant the whole complex of home life. It is obvious that the first telegram was written in part by Rogash of whom I wrote earlier and whose portrait is included.

The most crucial moments are frequently reflected in M.A.'s joking notes. When civic death, that is complete annihilation of the writer Bulgakov, became unbearable, he decided to appeal to the government, or rather to Stalin. I have before me the following notes:

"Do not be deje... I'll fig..." is written on one. And on the other one: "Daddy found the solution. And he decided..."

What purports to be a copy of M.A.'s letter to the government is now circulating in Moscow. I hasten to point out that this "essay" of six pages has nothing in common with the original.

I cannot understand who profits from putting this "opus" in circulation. To begin with, the fact is that the original was first of all short. Secondly, he did not ask to go abroad. Thirdly, there were no high-faluting expressions in the letter, nor any philosophical generalizations. The basic idea of Bulgakov's letter was very simple.

"Give the writer a chance to write. By proclaiming his civic death you are pushing him toward the most extreme measures."

Let us recall the chronicle of events:

In 1925 the poet Sergei Esenin died, a suicide.

In 1926 the writer Andrei Sobol committed suicide.

In April 1930, when Bulgakov's appeal, sent at the end of March, was already in Stalin's hands, Vladimir Mayakovsky shot himself. Would it not have been a fine state of affairs if Mikhail Bulgakov had laid hands on himself the same year?

Stalin's archive, which I am convinced is still in perfect order, would certainly be very helpful in establishing the truth and in putting an end to these kind of "essays."

The "letter" which is now passing from hand to hand is a rather free and easy compilation of truth and fabrication, an obvious case of an intolerable distortion of historical truth. One can easily imagine that an intelligent man would hesitate for a long time before addressing himself to the "terrible spirit" as follows:

"I have been described as a 'literary janitor' who collects leftovers after a dozen guests have vomited."

One would have to be insane to quote things like that in a letter to the government, but M.A. was quite sane, intelligent and well bred... The telephone rang quite unexpectedly. It was Stalin's secretary Tovstukha, calling from the Central Party Committee. I answered the telephone and called M.A., and then I busied myself with housework. M.A. took the receiver and shortly thereafter he shouted "Lyubasha" so loudly and nervously that I rushed headlong to the telephone (we had an extension).

It was Stalin on the line. He spoke in a muffled voice and had a noticeable Georgian accent, and he spoke of himself in the third person. "Stalin received, Stalin read..." (He often liked to speak about himself in the third person.) He made this suggestion to Bulgakov: "Perhaps you would like to go abroad?"

A direct result of this conversation with Stalin was Bulgakov's assignment to work at the Theater of Young Workers, abbreviated as TRAM.

Soon after this two young people appeared at our house on Pirogovsky. One was arrogant—Knorre; the other one was better behaved—Nikolai Kryuchkov. TRAM was not the Art Theater where M.A. was longing to be employed, but he could not afford to be fussy. The TRAM company went to the Crimea and asked Bulgakov to come with them. He went.

July 15, 1930. Morning. Near Kursk.

Well, Lyubanya, you can be happy now that I left. You miss me of course. By the way, there ought to be a telegram from the theater in Leningrad. Wire me briefly what the theater offers me. I will apparently find out my address when we get to Sevastopol. Honey, please go by the tailors. Open all the mail. Yours.

The boisterous energy of the TRAM people sent them hunting all over the train, and they brought back the news that there was room in first class. In Serpukhov I paid extra and moved there.

In the Serpukhov buffet there was not a drop of any kind of liquid. Just imagine the TRAM people with a guitar, without pillows, without tea pots, without water, on wooden shelves. I suppose they will be corpses in the morning. I set up housekeeping on the top shelf. With revulsion I admire the landscape. Sun. Geese.

July 16, 1930. Near Simferopol. Morning.

Dear Lyubanya. There is bright sunshine here. The Crimea is as repulsive as it used to be. The TRAM people are fit as fiddles. Now and then one can come across something at the station buffets, but mostly they are quite empty. Farm women in the South bring cucumbers, cherries, eggs, buns, onions, and milk to the train. The train is running late. I saw Olenka in Kharkov (she is very nice, brought me cigarettes), Fedya, Komissarov and Leslie. They came out to the train. I kiss you. How is Bouton?

Please my angel, go to Bychkov the tailor so he can take care of my suit. I will be measured when I arrive. If there is a telegram from the theater in Leningrad, send me a telegram. M.

July 17, 1930. The Crimea. Miskhor. "Magnolia" Pension.

Dear Lyubinka, I am settled nicely here. The weather is indescribably beautiful. I regret very much that none of my friends are here, all strange faces.* The food— privately there doesn't seem to be a damned thing. With the full pension plan it is entirely satisfactory. It is too bad that I could not bring you (my conscience is bothering me because I am alone in the sun). Now I am going to Yalta in a motor launch; I want to see what is there. Greetings to all. I kiss you. Maka.

*But the TRAM people were nice.

I will explain the letter of July 16: Olenka is Olga Bokshanskaya, V.I. Nemirovich-Danchenko's secretary. Fedya is Fedor Mikhalsky, the manager of the Art Theater. Komissarov and Leslie are actors at that theater.

Soon after M.A.'s arrival in the Crimea he received a summons from the Central Committee of the Party, but the paper seemed suspect to Bulgakov. It turned out to be one of Yury Olesha's "nice jokes." In general, Stalin's telephone call was widely commented on in Moscow. Each person added his own little mite of invention, which they continue to do to this day.

And so the romance with the Theater for Working Youth did not materialize. M.A. was assigned the job at the Art Theater, a job which he had been trying ardently to obtain.

In the evenings the writer Natalya Venkstern often came to see us. She had already written the play *In 1825*, which had a successful run on the second stage of MXAT. Giatsintova and Bersenev were especially good in it. The Moscow Art Theater asked her to write a stage version of Dickens' *Pickwick Club*. Then rumors went around Moscow that it was Bulgakov who wrote the play. This was not true; Moscow loves to gossip.

Natasha brought finished portions in which she had conscientiously tried to retain Dickens' long sentences, but with lightning speed M.A. divided them into short dialogues suited to the stage. It was very interesting to observe this magic transformation. But Natalya Venkstern, a very intelligent and capable woman, caught on very quickly to what Bulgakov was trying to do.

The Pickwick Club was produced at MXAT in 1934 by Stanitsyn. The scenery in the style of old colored prints was painted by Peter Vilyams and the music was by N. Sizov. Some of the songs still sound in my memory: "Hello, my home, / Farewell to the road" was sung many times by the Muscovites. In 1935, M.A. appeared in the play in the role of the judge. This was the only role that he ever played at MXAT. The public loved the youthful show; it was effervescent, full of life. I believe the play would still be of interest and would even be of use to young people as an example of an English classic.

At that time of crisis I tried to find a job. At my driver's education course I had already been offered a job by the engineer Boris Shprink at his editorial office. He was working as the associate of the chief editor of the *Technical Encyclopedia*. I accepted. I liked it. Everybody was very cultured and it was easy to breathe there.

"Well, Lyubasha, nothing will come of all this," said M.A. He apparently felt acutely the current hostility against himself, the writer Bulgakov, and thought that it would also rub off on me, his wife.

It was as if he were looking into clear water. The prescribed month before I would be accepted on the staff went by; only a few days were left. Shprink called me into his office and told me with some embarrassment the the Personnel Department would not accept me: "Ludvig Karlovich himself [that is Martens, the chief editor] has spoken with personnel; he insisted that they accept you and tried to convince them, but all in vain."

I thanked him and went back to Pirogovsky. I did not know then who Ludvig Martens was. I knew that he was a cultured, well-educated and kind man. Thirty-five years went by. And now I have before me *Izvestiya* of January 19, 1965. The headline reads: "Fighters for the Great Goal." A portrait. The title is: "Diplomat, Scholar, Inventor." The short biography

Bulgakov in 1928. Inscribed: "To my dear Lyubasha, from Tu. To. K."

tells that Ludvig Martens was a staunch Bolshevik-Leninist and an advisor to Vladimir Ilich; he had carried out revolutionary assignments in Germany and England for Lenin himself. In 1919, on Lenin's order and by the decision of the Central Party Committee, Martens was appointed the representative of the Soviet Government to the United States, where he spent two stormy and difficult years. He was nevertheless able to organize a Soviet Mission in New York and to found two societies: The Friends of Soviet Russia, and Technical Assistance to Soviet Russia. When he returned to Moscow a friendly meeting took place between him and V.I. Lenin in the latter's Kremlin apartment. Ludvig Martens played a great part in organizing the economy and technology of the young Soviet republic. He was a member of the presidium of the State Planning Commission and a chancellor and professor at the Lomonosov Technical Institute in Moscow. He had scientific works and inventions to his credit... It is nice for me to know that such a man had interceded for me.

But the personnel department turned out to be stronger than the distinguished advisor to Lenin!

In 1931 Vsevolod Meyerhold invited M.A. to come and talk to him at the theater. Six years went by and Meyerhold had apparently had time to forget what was written in Bulgakov's story "The Fatal Eggs" (in the collection *Diaboliad*, 1925, p. 79):

"Over the theater of the late Vsevolod Meyerhold, who died, as everyone knows, in 1927, during the staging of Pushkin's *Boris Godunov*, when a platform full of naked boyars collapsed on him, there flashed a moving multicolored neon sign promulgating the writer Erendorg's play, *Chicken Croak*..." Meyerhold had forgotten, but the writer Erenburg did not forget or forgive this *Chicken Croak*.

It was not only in *Diaboliad* that M.A. Bulgakov carried on polemics against the artistic style of Meyerhold's theatrical direction. I have in from of the author's feuilleton "The Capital in a Notebook," printed in the newspaper *On the Eve* on February 9, 1923. There is a section VI entitled: "Biomechanical Chapter." I will quote an excerpt from it:

Call me Vandal.
I deserve that name.

I admit that before I wrote those lines I hesitated for a long time. I was afraid. Then I decided to risk it.

After I had become convinced that The Hugenots *and* Rigoletto *had ceased to entertain me, I abruptly rushed over to the left front. The reason for this was I. Ehrenburg, who had written the book* And It Goes On Turning *and also two long-haired Moscow Futurists who came to me every day for a week, and while drinking evening tea they scolded me for my "petit bourgeois mentality."*

It is not nice when these words hit you in the face, so I went, damn them! I went to the State Institute for Dramatic Arts Theater to see The Magnanimous Cuckold, *produced by Meyerhold.*

The problem is this: I am a working man. I earn each million through sleepless nights and days of running around like an animal. The little money I have—is the kind that is called blood money. For me the theater is enjoyment, peace, entertainment, in a word anything at all except a way to contract another nice case of neurasthenia, especially since there are dozens of ways to contract it in Moscow without spending money for a ticket to the theater.

I am not Ehrenburg, and not a wise theater critic, but judge for yourselves. In a bare and ragged theater there is a hole instead of a stage (there is not even a trace of a curtain, of course). At the far end there is a brick wall with two sepulchral windows. There is a structure in front of the wall. Compared to it a design by Tatlin could be considered a model of clarity and simplicity. Some kind of cages, sloping planes, sticks, little doors and wheels. And on the wheels there are the letters SCH and TE upside down. The theater's carpenters walk back and forth as if they are at home, and for a long time it is impossible to understand whether or not the play has started.

When it does start (you know it does, because a light flashes onto the stage from the side somewhere) dark blue people appear (actors and actresses, all in dark blue).

The action; a woman, tucking in her blue skirt,

slides down an inclined plane to where a woman and a man are sitting. The woman is brushing off the man's back with a clothes brush. The woman rides on the man's shoulders, modestly covering her legs with her factory worker's skirt.

This is biomechanics, my friend explains to me.

Biomechanics!! The feebleness of these dark blue blue biomechanics who had at one time learned to deliver sickly sweet monologues, is beyond compare. And please note that this is next door to the Nikitin Circus where the clown Lazarenko stuns the audience with awesome somersaults.

They dejectedly and persistently keep hitting someone with a swinging door in the same place again and again. The mood in the audience is like the mood in a graveyard near the grave of someone's beloved wife. The wheels turn and squeak.

After the first act the usher says: "Don't you like it here, sir?"

Such an insolent smile that I desperately wanted to box his ears.

Meyerhold is a genius, howled the Futurist.

I am not going to argue about that. It is very possible. So be it—a genius. It's all the same to me. But we must not forget that genius is unique, and I am the crowd. I am the spectator. The theater is for me. I want to go to a theater which I can understand.

When we arrived at Meyerhold's theater they were giving Yury Olesha's new play *The List of Assets*. He was at the performance. I remember that the play was very good, but in the last act it was not quite clear why the heroine, played by Zinaida Raikh, suddenly dies. (By a stray bullet from a Paris *agent de police*, Olesha explained to us.)

We went backstage to see Meyerhold. Never in my life had I seen such an uninviting theater; in fact I even find it unpleasant to remember it. In 1927 it was the scene of a public dispute about the production of *The Days of the Turbins* and Trenev's *Liubov Yarovaia*. Of the two "memoirists"—Ermolinsky and Mindlin—the latter comes nearer the truth if only because he mentions that M.A. behaved with dignity; he did not choke, did not wave his arms and did not yell at all, as Ermolinsky reports about this incident (in the journal *Theater*, No. 6, 1966).

The journal *Ogonyok* has published excerpts of the stenographic record of this dispute (No. 2, March 1969).

M.A. spoke impromptu, and for that reason not very smoothly; but the main idea of this presentation was clear, and Bulgakov's persistent persecutor Orlinsky got his smack in the nose.

I could easily imagine how convictions were obtained from heretics in the old days when the Grand Inquisitor was presiding... We must give my poor heretic his due—he was on top.

I would like to mention in passing a few words about Yury Olesha. When his book *No Day Without a Line* came out in 1965 I eagerly set out to read it in the secret hope of finding even a few lines about Bulgakov in it. They did work together for a long time; their plays were performed at the same theater, Olesha used to visit us, M.A. called him "kid" and took the "joke" with indulgence when Olesha played the trick of sending him a summons to the Central Committee. Who if not Olesha, would be obliged to mention M.A., for the logical reason that they were in the same situation! But no, there was not a single line. Why? Because of a zealous editor? Somehow I do not believe that the name of the writer Bulgakov was not mentioned a single time in the manuscript.

In the preface the modesty of the book's author is noted. I quote: "When they rehearse this play I see how well written *The List of Assets* actually is. In this connection I can even use the phrase, 'What a remarkable work...'"

And further: "I am convinced that I wrote a book (*Envy*) which will live for a century. I have kept the draft of it which I wrote in longhand. There is an emanation of refinement from these sheets. That is how I speak of myself."

And one last quote which follows an argument with a newspaper vendor at a news stand: "Did I ever think as a boy when I was playing soccer, did I think that I, a famous writer at whom, by the way, the entire theater turned around to look, could I imagine that on a hot summer's day I would walk away from a news stand, driven away, and for a reason."

Chekhov would never have written like that. Bulgakov

would never have written like that either.

Is that really modesty?

The year 1931 was primarily noted for the work on *Dead Souls* which M.A. was adapting for the stage of the Art Theater. Since he felt the dramatist had to have some degree of latitude, he did not approach this work by a writer whom he worshipped with as much academic respect as the theater required. And so he presented another variant that he himself favored, or rather, a plan for a variant: *Gogol in Rome*. In it Gogol assumes the main role of narrator; he directs the performance. M.A. wrote enthusiastically; he imagined to himself how it would sound and look on stage. The text was almost entirely taken from Gogol; it was put together in a masterly fashion. But Stanislavsky did not agree with Bulgakov and adopted instead the "academic" variant.

Maka was very bitter and kept saying again and again: "Too bad about Rome! Where is my Rome?"

Bulgakov not only dramatized *Dead Souls*, but he also took part in the production as assistant to the director.

In 1932 *Dead Souls* saw the footlights. The leading roles were distributed as follows:

I. M. Moskvin — Nozdrev
I. M. Tarkhanov — Sobakevich
L. M. Leonidov — Plyushkin
V. O. Toporkov — Chichikov
M. P. Lilina — Korobochka
M. N. Kedrov — Malinov
V. Ya. Stanitsyn — the governor

One day soon after the opening night the telephone rang. M.A. went to the telephone, said a couple of words, put down the receiver and turned to me.

"Konstantin Sergeevich [Stanislavsky] wants to talk to you."

I made negative signs with my hands and shook my head, but no, there was nothing I could do but talk to him.

"Was the show interesting?" asked K.S.

I answered in the affirmative but with some slight restraint. The unusual old man could apparently sense that something was amiss. He said, "Don't hesitate to tell the truth. I wouldn't like the play to resemble textbook illustrations."

I did not tell K.S. that it was exactly textbook illustrations that this play reminded me of, and of the Alexandrinka Theater in Petrograd, where we were taken to see performances of the classics...

Now that I have a chance to recall the bygone years of our eventful life, I want to talk in more detail about some traits of M.A.'s character. —He was kindhearted in a bashful way; he did not want it to be advertised when he had done something good. There was this incident: We were informed that our friend Elena Lansberg had started labor and that she was having a difficult time; she was suffering terribly. Without saying a word, Maka immediately went to her. Elena herself remembered the rest, many years later, after M.A.'s death:

"He came completely unexpectedly; he was particularly tender and tried so hard to calm me that I had to calm down if only from a feeling of simple gratitude. But joking aside, he dragged me out of the region of black despair and gave me the strength to bear the rest of the suffering. There was something hypnotizing in his calming words, and because of that I will remember how he helped me during those difficult days for the rest of my life."

In later years a distant relative of M.A.'s first wife, Tatyana Lappa, got in the habit of coming to see us. This girl's name was Manya, and in many ways she was a strange creature with whom you had to be on your guard. She worked in a factory where she did not get along with the management. To spite them she went off into such hysterics (I can just imagine) that they sent her to a mental hospital. Actually, the doctor realized after a few days that it was simulation and sent her home. M.A. asked her what she was hoping to gain by playing such tricks. "I was counting on you," she replied without blinking an eye. "I knew that you would help me no matter what might have happened."

On the whole she was a worthless wench, but she did not for a moment of doubt M. A.'s kindness...

M.A. loved animals, but it was I who had "infected" him. I am glad that I introduced a completely new theme into the writer's work. I have in mind how my inclination, or rather my constant and unchanging love for animals, is reflected in his works.

His entire literary path is before me. Nowhere, never (except for the column "The Talking Dog" printed in the newspaper *The Whistle (Gudok)*, but that dog was the object of fraud) did he dwell on descriptions of a domestic cat or a favorite dog; there simply were not any, just as there were not any at all to be found in the Bulgakovs' home in Kiev. Let us turn to the novel *The White Guard*. A spacious house, comfortable furniture, a closely knit family. It would seem that there ought to be a housecat living there, curled up in the old arm chair. But no. It could not be like that here.

And then I turn up, and various animals are always huddling around me, and I am always feeding them.

Then, in 1925 the tale *Heart of a Dog* (dedicated to me), was written in our first home together. The hero of the story, the stray dog Sharik, is described with penetrating sympathy. Our next home on Maly Levshinsky Lane was "equipped with" the cat Muka. She is praised in the manuscript book *Muka-Maka* (poems by V.D., illustrations by N. Ushakova and S. Topleninov). In the chapter "Neurasthenia" in M.A.'s last unfinished work, *Theatrical Novel*, the narrator Maxudov is the victim of a fear of death. In his solitude he seeks "help and protection from death. And I found this help. There was a soft miau from the cat that I had earlier picked up at the gate. The animal became worried. After a second the animal was already sitting on the newspapers, looking at me with his round eyes, asking what was going on. The smoke-colored, scraggly animal was concerned that nothing should happen. In fact, who was going to feed this old cat?

This was an attack of neurasthenia, I explained to the cat. It had already taken hold of me, it would develop and consume me. But in the meantime I could go on living for a while..."

The next stage was the dog Bouton (named in honor of Molière's servant).

We moved to a separate three-room apartment on Bolshoi Pirogovsky where Bouton would reign.

In the sequence with Voland in the novel *The Master and Margarita*, the magic and mischievous cat Behemoth is described. He is, according to the author himself, "the best jester who ever existed in the world." Our mischievous and enchanting kitten

Flyushka served as model for him.

In the same novel (in the chapters written with unsurpassed mastery) the procurator of Judea, the knight and patrician Pontius Pilate, has a favorite dog, Banga. At the turning point in the interrogation of Yeshua the procurator's headache goes away and Yeshua says to Pilate, "You can only long for your dog, who is clearly the only creature for whom you have any affection."

In the play *Adam and Eve* (1931), even in the midst of a world-wide catastrophe the academician Efrosimov, a chemist and inventor of an apparatus that neutralizes the most terrible gases, grieves that he does not have time to irradiate his only friend, the dog Jack, and thus prevent his death.

Efrosimov: "Oh, if it were not for Jack I would be completely alone in this world, because I cannot count my aunt who irons my shirt. Jack brings light into my life. Jack, my dog. I saw four kids carrying a puppy and laughing. It seemed that they were going to hang it. But I paid them twelve rubles, so that they would not hang him. Now he has grown up, and I am never parted from him. On days when there is no poison he sits in my laboratory and watches me work. Why should anyone want to hang a dog?"

We were often late and always in a hurry. Sometimes we had to run after buses or trolleys. But M.A. invariably said, "The main thing is not to lose one's dignity."

When I go over in my memory the years that I lived with him I can say that this phrase, sometimes pronounced in jest, was also the writer Bulgakov's credo all during his life.

Cover and drawing from *Muka-Maki* a comic book about the Bulgakov's, illustrated by Ushakova.

L. B. Baratov and Bulgakov, 1928(?).

SOME THOUGHTS ABOUT THE THEATER
OF THOSE YEARS

I will end my memoirs with a short chapter about art and Bulgakov's work in the theater during those years. Of course I do not pretend to give an exhaustive analysis. The recent official changes in relation to the writer's works obviously gladden me, but my memory—"the evil master"—brings me back against my will to those years.

I remember that the album of clippings of various reviews gradually swelled up and that M.A.'s stoical attitude towards it gradually grew weaker. The writer's nervous system grew weaker at the same time; he became more irritable and suspicious, started to sleep badly and developed a twitch in his shoulder and head (a nervous tic).

It is actually surprising that his explosive creativity did not dry up because of these constant rude and abusive articles. I would have preferred to say "critical articles," but I cannot— I am not able to form the words...

"I do not believe in hiding one's light under a bushel," is one of M.A. Bulgakov's expressions. "Sooner or later the writer will say what he wants to say in spite of everything." These words of his are directly connected with the expression from the Gospels: "Neither do men light a candle, and put it under a bushel, but on a candle stick; and it giveth light unto all that are in the house" (Matthew 5:15).

And in fact, creative thought lives and shines. And manuscripts do not burn.

The play *Flight* was written in great enthusiasm in these years (1928). Our literary critics completely arbitrarily call it the sequel to *The Days of the Turbins*. M.A. himself never regarded it as a sequel to *The Days of the Turbins*. Although the play was dedicated to the principal performers of *The Turbins*, and although he dreamed of seeing them on stage in *Flight*, the dramatic ring of his work is nevertheless completely different; the tuning fork gives off a different key. The dramatist's grasp has been strengthened, his taste has become more precise, the writer's scope has widened, and his painter's palette has blossomed out in new colors. In *The Days of the Turbins* the beginning of the White movement is shown, in *Flight* the end of it. In this way the second play continues the first one, only in time. It is not part of my task, however, to enter into polemics with those who think otherwise. *Flight* is my favorite play and I consider it to be a play of unusual power, the most important and interesting of all of Bulgakov's dramatic works.

Unfortunately, I do not remember now which military sources besides General Slashchov's memoirs (Ya. A. Slashchov, *The Crimea in 1920. Excerpts From His Memoirs With a Preface by D. Furmanov.* Moscow, 1924) M. A. used as he worked on *Flight.* I do remember that all the military movements of the Red and White troops were shown on one of the maps, and tiny inhabited locations were shown as they are supposed to be on military maps.

We spread out the map, and after checking it against the text of the book, we drew the path of the Red advance and the White retreat; it is for this reason that the play includes so many genuine place names connected with historical battles and movements of troops: Perekop, Sivash, Chongar, Kurchulan, Almanayka, Baby Yar, The Arbatskaya Arrow, Taganash, Yushun, Kerman-Kemalchi...

So as to "breathe" the atmosphere of Constantinople, where I had spent several months, M.A. asked me to tell him about the city. I told him, and like an artist he took only the very brightest spots that he needed for his stage representation.

The shouts, the bustle, the international crowd of a large Eastern city are shown very expressively and correctly. (I want to point out that Constantinople was then under the administration of France, England and Italy. Internal order was maintained by an international police force. The Sultan still existed nominally; but on the opposite side of the Bosporus, on the Asian side, Kemal was already shooting.)

As for the "cockroach races," they were developed by Bulgakov with his extraordinary brilliance and fantasy from Arkady Averchenko's story "The Constantinople Menagerie," where the author imparts his impressions of the Constantinople of those years. There really were no cockroach races, of course. They were only a bitter hyperbole and symbol—the only thing left for the emigrant was a cockroach race.

I told M.A. about the most varied meetings, events, and experiences from the years preceding our marriage. He found them interesting, and in his own handwriting he used my stories to outline a book which I didn't write then, but which I am now writing. I am afraid that his outline plan does not remain among his papers.

M.A. paid special attention to my oral portrait of Vladimir Krymov, the Petersburg man of letters. My description somehow interested the writer, and passed through his creative laboratory. It took the form of the caricature—the portrait of Paramon Korzukhin in *Flight*.

V.P. Krymov was editor and co-publisher of the Petersburg journal *Capital and Country Home*, and the author of a rather good book entitled *Pilgrims in My Basket*, where he tells of his impressions from a journey around the world. He came from a family of Siberian Old Believers. He left Russia as soon as it began to smell of revolution: "When grouse in a restaurant started to cost sixty kopeks instead of forty, it indicated that things were not satisfactory in the country." His own words. As he was a wealthy man, he had acquired real estate in almost every European country, even in Honolulu...

The scene showing Korzukhin in Paris was written under the influence of my account of how I beat everyone at cards when I sat down to play "ten" with Krymov and his group (for the first time in my life). He did not allow female servants. The ex-soldier Klimenko was employed in the house. In the play, the butler is called Antoine Grishchenko.

In a note characterizing Khludov the author writes, "Khludov is snub-nosed, like Pavel." This refers most likely to Khmelev who was, in fact, snub-nosed, not to Khludov's prototype Slashchov. Those who had seen the general said that he was quite handsome.

M.A. and I delighted in the thought of what Khmelev, with his limitless capabilities, would make of this role. The Moscow Art Theater accepted the play and began to rehearse.

The principal roles were, in our minds, distributed as follows:

                Khludov — N.P. Khmelev
                Charnota — B.G. Dobronravov
                Serafima — V.S. Sokolova
                Lyuska — O.N. Androvskaya
                Golubkov — M.M. Yanshin

Korzukhin — ?
Afrikan — ?
Vrangel — Maloletkov

It was a terrible blow when it was banned. As if a corpse had started to haunt the house...

In 1959 I went to a performance of my favorite play at the Pushkin Academic Theater in Leningrad. I liked neither the production nor the acting. Cherkasov, who played Khludov, attempted to represent an officer of the guard and had adopted a peculiar kind of "Odessa accent." Charnota looked like Taras Bulba, and Constantinople did not look like Constantinople. (It was produced by the People's Artist L.S. Viven and the scenery was by the Honored Artist of the RSFSR A.F. Bosulaev.) The play did not have the "hellish" success that Gorky had predicted.

The year 1929. The play *Molière: A Cabal of Hypocrites*, is being written. The same creative instinct is still at work, not yet killed nor finished off. I have just translated a biography of Molière from the French. I remember the long triumphant poem where creativity is identified with the forces and beauties of nature...

M.A. walks around his study, dictates the text, playing this or that part as he goes along. His acting is very entertaining.

I like the way the French write biographies. They include many vivid details, which give the playwright many dramatic colors. I remember the taste and skill with which the author, a true Frenchman, described Armande's toilette: a yellow silk gown trimmed with white lace...

I can see before me M.A.'s not very handsome, but talented face as he declaims somewhat nasally: "Muse, my muse, oh, fickle Thalia..."

And then the play was finished. The first reading was held at the Lyamins'. At the second reading, held at our home on Pirogovsky, O. L. Knipper-Chekhov, I. M. Moskvin, V. Ya. Stanitsyn, M.M. Yanshin, P.A. Markov and the Lyamins were present. Candles were burning in the candleabra on M.A.'s desk He read brilliantly, as always.

The opening night was at the MXAT on February 15, 1936.

The director was Gorchakov, Assistants to the director were M.A. Bulgakov, B.N. Livanov, and V.V. Protasevich. The music was by R.M. Gliere. The artist was P.V. Vilyams.

The principal roles were as follows:

Jean Baptiste Poquelin de Molière, great playwright and actor — V. Ya. Stanitsyn.

Madeleine Béjart, Molière's first wife, actress — L.M. Koreneva.

Armande Béjart, her sister, later Molière's second wife, actress —A.O. Stepanova.

La Grange, actor and the secretary of Molière's theater — B.N. Livanov

Bouton, lamplighter at Molière's theater and his personal servant — M. Yanshin.

Louis XIV, King of France — M.P. Bolduman.

Marquis d'Orsini, captain of the black musketeers — N.A. Podgorny.

Archbishop of Paris, Marquis de Charron — N.N. Sosin.

The work did not bring M.A. much luck. After several performances the play was removed from the repertory. I did not see that production, but I am quite sure that at MXAT there could not have been any of the jeers that the play is now having to endure at the theater of the Lenin Komsomol.

I resisted for a long time and did not go to see A.V. Efros' production of *Molière*; his "revision" of *The Seagull* was quite enough for me. But I was given a ticket as a name-day present, and I really couldn't refuse it and not go.

The play was originally dedicated to me. But I did not imagine that they were expecting me.

To begin with, not every dramatic text lends itself to a purely conventional interpretation where the spectator himself must keep on racking his brains, trying to guess who is who, who is where, and why it is as it is...

For instance, how should the spectator be able to understand that it is Louis XIV, the "Sun of France," who is making his way amidst the props thrown about the theater at random. The actor himself could hardly believe that he was portraying this "Sun." Nor did we, the spectators, believe it.

Why, in the last act, does the leading actress of the Paris (yes, Paris) theater, Madeleine Bejart, look like a favorite from the Moscow district dressed in a loose jacket? Why does the other actress, Armande Bejart, later Moliere's wife, behave in such a vulgar way? The interpretation of conventions is a discriminating process, and even if the spectator accepts the conventions that have become established over centuries in the Japanese kabuki theater, then A. V. Efros' way of doing things backwards does not make for a very tasteful show. I will openly admit that I suffered all during the show, and I left the theater with a bitter feeling of resentment on behalf of M. A., whose talent was at moments able to break through the director's shell. Then at once it became interesting and lighthearted.

The composer Andrei Volkonsky, who was usually a man of good taste, and who moreover spent his whole youth in France, contributed to the general muddle of this production.

And here is the basic thought that came to me. Let us imagine that Bulgakov is crossing a wide street where and when it is permitted, but Efros comes rushing along on his motorcycle. Since he is not paying attention to the traffic lights, he knocks Bulgakov down and cripples him. He must answer for it according to the stern Soviet laws—that is what lawyers and logic tell me. So why is nobody held responsible for morally crippling a writer's works? Why?

In 1962 M.A. Bulgakov's biography of Molière came out in the series "Lives of Remarkable People." Thirty years after it was written.

After having read Bulgakov's manuscript at that time, the founder of the series, Gorky, said to the chief editor Alexander Tikhonov (Serebrov), "I must admit that it shows talent. But if we start to print books like that, then we are going to be in trouble."

I was then working at ZhZL (Lives of Remarkable People) and A.N. Tikhonov, who had always treated me as a friend, told me immediately about Gorky's opinion.

In the commentary on page 138 of the Molière biography, Professor G. Boyadzhiev has reproached Bulgakov for focussing attention on the suspicions about Molière's supposed fatherhood;

namely that Armande Béjart, his wife, was his own daughter by Madeleine Béjart. Enemies of the great writer, writes Professor Boyadzhiev, have accused him of contracting an incestuous marriage. Recent scientific research concerning Molière rejects this slander.

But I have here in front of me the newspaper *L'Humanite* of June 2, 1963, which certainly cannot be suspected of hostility towards Molière. I am reading the headline: "Does Armande Béjart Need Acquittal?" In 1663 a marriage service was held in the church of Saint Germain Auxerrois between Jean-Baptiste Poquelin, called Molière, and Armande Béjart. She had created the major female roles in the great writer's works. These roles are said to have been written especially for her and reflect many of her characteristic features: Elise in *Critique of the School for Wives,* Elmire in *Tartuffe,* Célimène in *The Misanthrope* and Elise in *The Miser.*

The name of Armande Béjart is connected with many mysteries; was she the sister or daughter of Madeleine Béjart, the beloved joint owner of Molière's theater? Or Poquelin's own daughter? Did she make Molière unhappy or was it the other way around; did the elderly, sick, and jealous husband make her life unbearable? Jean Berger and Mme. Chevalley attempt to answer all these questions in their report which they have entitled 'Famous Names of the Past,' given in the house in Medon where Armande Béjart lived after the death of her husband."

M.A. Bulgakov wrote his *Molière* in 1932-1933, but thirty years later the French are still debating the question in public of whether Armande Béjart was the daughter of the famous playwright. One can conclude from this that the opinion officially accepted by Molière scholars is not necessarily shared by the French themselves.

In the same sweeping creative stretch during which he wrote *Flight,* he also wrote the fantastic play *Adam and Eve,* in 1931.

The author prefaced his play with a quote from the work *Military Gases*: "The fate of the daredevils who thought that gas was nothing to be afraid of was always the same—death." And then to soften the grim impression he added another, more peaceful quote from the Bible: "Neither will I ever again destroy every living creature as I have done. While the earth remains, seedtime and harvest shall not cease" (Gen. 8:21-22).

The academician Efrosimov, professor of chemistry, had constructed the apparatus which neutralizes the effects of the most terrible and most destructive gases. His invention can save mankind from destruction. Profound pacificism is a characteristic trait of Academician Efrosimov. The following dialogue is indicative of this.

Professor, you were saying that it is possible to make an invention that would eliminate chemical warfare.

EFROSIMOV: Yes.

DARAGAN: Amazing. You were even asking whom to give it to.

EFROSIMOV: Yes, alas. It is an agonizing question. I suppose that in order to save mankind from destruction it will be necessary to give this invention to all countries at the same time...

But the academician's pacifism not only does not meet with sympathy from those around him, on the contrary, it provokes suspicion and gives rise to the thought that he may be a traitor.

The catastrophe is unavoidable all the same. The carpenter, who is making a carrying case for the apparatus, brings it too late.

Against the background of a worldwide catastrophe various destinies and characters come into conflict.

M.A. read the play at the Vakhtangov Theater the same year. The people at the Vakhtangov, who were great diplomats, invited Alksnis, the head of the Soviet Air Force, to the reading. He said that the play could not be produced, because Leningrad is destroyed during the course of the action.

Of course, it was possible to approach this work with other criteria, if one wanted to. First one could change the name of the city, and second, one must keep in mind that it is a work of fiction, which can create and destroy (which is what made it fantasy) entire worlds, entire planets.

The first version of "The Consultant With a Hoof" was written in 1928 also here on Bolshoi Pirogovsky. It was the basis for the novel *The Master and Margarita*. As far as I remember, "The Consultant" was more selective, more harmonious; there was less deviltry, although the same Voland and his companion the magic cat were still in command of the events in Moscow. Voland started out from the Patriarchs Ponds too, although it was not Annushka, but Pelageyushka who spilled the fateful lenten butter on the street-car tracks. The scene showing Yeshua's execution was as wonderfully and subtly described as it was in the subsequent variants of the novel.

Among scenes from everyday life, the auction in a former church was very memorable. A former church deacon conducts the auction, and he sells the former tsar's fur coat...

A few lines from *The Master and Margarita* pierced me forever, right to the heart: "Gods, my gods! How sad the world is in the evening! How mysterious the mists over the swamps! He will know it who has wandered astray in those mists, who has suffered greatly before dying, who has flown here over this earth bearing an unbearable burden. He knows it, too, who is exhausted. And without regret he leaves the mists of the earth, its swamps and its rivers, with a light heart he gives himself into the arms of death, knowing that death alone will comfort him."

These lines, a mournful sigh, are always with me. Even now they move me to tears...

In the description of Mikhail Bulgakov's archive (No. 37 of *Notes of the Manuscript Division*, Lenin Library, 1976) all the variants of the novel *The Master and Margarita* are carefully examined; that is, the history of its writing. It is, however, pointed out that "nothing is known to us about the origin of the idea for the second novel."

Here is what I am able to tell about this. When we got to know N.N. Lyamin and his wife, the artist N.A. Ushakova, she gave M.A. a little book for which she had designed the cover, the frontispiece illustration "The Black Carriage" and the endpieces. This was *Venediktov; or, Memorable Events in My Life. A Romantic Tale, Written by the Botanist X; Illustrated by the Phytopathologist Y.* Moscow, In the year V of the Republic. On the title page: "Dedicated to the newborn dream." Then: RVTs; Moscow, No. 818. Printed in 1000 copies. The first Model Press of MSNKh. 71, Pyatnitskaya.

The author, who does not reveal himself anywhere in the book, was Professor A.V. Chayanov.

When she illustrated the book, Ushakova was astounded to see that the hero who tells the entire story has the name Bulgakov. M.A. was no less astounded by this coincidence.

The entire narrative is concerned with Satan's presence in Moscow and with Bulgakov's struggle for the soul of his beloved, who has fallen under the power of the Devil. Chayanov's story is complicated; it is teeming with unusual events. The narrator, Bulgakov, suddenly feels an extraordinary oppression on his soul. "It seemed that somebody's heavy hand was pressing down on my brain, shattering the bony covering of the skull..." Thus, the narrator experiences the presence of the Devil.

Satan in Moscow. His meeting with Bulgakov takes place in the Medox theater...

The charming actress on stage looks intently into the darkness of the audience "with an expression of submission and mental agony." The woman makes a profound impression on Bulgakov; she becomes his dream, the meaning of his life.

Before whom is it that the actress is trembling? "It was he... He was tall rather than short, wearing a gray, rather unfashionable coat; his hair was turning gray and his eyes, still fixed on the stage, were dim... There were no flames licking him, nor did it smell of brimstone; everything about him was commonplace and ordinary, but the demon's ordinariness was saturated with *significance and authority*" (the author's italics).

The hero is followed all around Moscow by a sinister-looking black carriage which is taking Nastenka (the heroine) to an unknown distant place... On the way he admires the sleepy city and especially "the gigantic Pashkov house the jutting top of which vanished upwards."

Fate causes Bulgakov and Venediktov to meet, and the latter tells of his demonic ability to gain complete possession of human minds.

"My power is limitless, Bulgakov," he says, "and my grief is limitless; the greater my power, the greater my grief." He tells of his stormy life, about a Black Mass, orgies, crimes and then, unexpectedly: " 'You don't understand anything, Bulgakov!' My frightening companion suddenly stopped in front of me.

'Do you know what is in that iron chest? Your soul is there, Bulgakov.' "But Bulgakov wins his soul back from Venediktov in a game of cards.

After many stormy events and after Venediktov's death, Nastenka's soul gains its freedom; Nastenka and Bulgakov, who have come to love each other, join their lives.

I can say with conviction that this little story gave M.A. the original idea and creative impulse for the novel *The Master and Margarita*.

It is easy to observe this by comparing the introduction of the first variant of the novel with the introduction to Chayanov's story. The reader's attention is involuntarily attracted by the similarities between their linguistic structures.

The author of the description of M.A.'s archives writes, "The novel began with an introduction by a narrator—a non-professional man who has taken up the pen with one single purpose—to describe events which had so astounded him."

We read in M.A. Bulgakov's work: "I swear by my honor... I am pierced as soon as I take up my pen to (describe monstrous) events (I am only worried) that since I am not (a writer) I will not be able to reproduce any of (these events).

Forget about them, however, the literary refinements; (I am not chasing after the ephemeral glories of the author) but I am very worried..."

Let us compare it with Chayanov's introduction:

"After spending many years in my rural solitude meditating over this, I reached the decision to follow the example of the philosopher from Chaeronea [Plutarch] and describe the life of an ordinary Russian man. Since I do not know any other life-style in any detail, and since I do not have access to a library, I decided, perhaps without suitable modesty, to proceed to describe the memorable events in my own life, assuming that many of these events will not be without interest to the readers."

Not only do they have an identical linguistic structure, but also the contents of the introductions are similar—the same fear that the author, a non-professional writer, will not be able to handle the description of the "memorable events" of his life. Both works are first-person.

I would like to make some observations about the prototype

of Fesya, the hero in the first variant of Chapter 11 of *The Master and Margarita* (p. 70, Note 108 in the same *Notes* No. 37).

The author of the study rather boldly points to N.N. Lyamin's old acquaintance (from his early years) Boris Yarkho as the prototype of Fesya. I think this statement is absolutely insupportable. To begin with, M.A. never showed any interest in Yarkho and never had any conversations—literary or otherwise—with Yarkho personally. Their interests and tastes never overlapped. Besides, they met very seldom, Yarkho was not present at all of M.A. Bulgakov's readings at the Lyamins'; and just as M.A. was not a frequent visitor at his house, he was not a frequent visitor at ours. I have talked to Natalya Ushakova about this. She agrees with me completely, recalling that Yarkho looked ridiculously spherical and spoke with a peculiar and funny kind of aspiration. No one denies that he possessed great erudition in many areas, including knowing almost twenty languages; but he has no connection with Fesya. I already explained elsewhere how the name of Fesya occurred to Bulgakov.

I would like to mention, even if briefly, the performances from those years, those which I almost always saw with M.A., or those which are memorable for other reasons.

Early in the spring of 1926 M.A. and I were able to experience an important theatrical event—the Bolshoi Opera's production of Rimsky-Korsakov's opera *The Legend of the Invisible City of Kitezh and the Maiden Fevronia.*

When M.A. listened to serious music that excited him he appeared to look different somehow—he even looked more handsome. I loved this expression on his face very much. Fevronia was sung by Derzhinskaya, Dirty Grishka by Ozerov, Suk conducted, and Korovin (who, by the way, was not credited at all) had painted the sets. What a lot of things started to happen after this production! The music critic Sergei Chemodanov insisted on the unquestionable merits of the opera (*Programs of the Academic Theaters*, No. 37, June 1926). He was supported by Sergei Boguslavsky, but Sadko (again that same old Sadko) chafed at the bit in his eagerness to discredit Rimsky-Korsakov's work: "Of all of Rimsky-Korsakov's operas only the three epochmaking operas (*Snow Maiden, Sadko* and *The Golden Cockerel*) are protected by the Academy. The rest are far from 'immortal.'

We must not go into protective raptures but we must keep our heads sober. In a word, it will not be a disaster or a loss to art if the government repudiates *Kitezh*, which is full of religious elements and only plays into the hands of private groups of believers" (*Life of Art*, No. 22, 1926).

And further the same Sadko speaks even more crudely: "Last Thursday the Radio Broadcasting Service broadcast from the Bolshoi Opera the religous opera *Kitezh*, which both in con- and music is nothing but a religious service. The broadcast was as usual accompanied by explanations pertaining to the music. The plot of the opera was expounded extremely unctuously and in great detail.

" 'The bells sound and the city becomes invisible,' the well-known voice of the apostle of the radio, the commentator S. Chemodanov, rings insistently over the air. Spinning a long yarn of popish lies the emotional music commentator makes the reservation in passing that..." and so on. And in conclusion the opera is called "*Kitezh*, opera of the priest-loving intelligentsia" (*Workers' Gazette*, No. 1).

Bulgakov was familiar with this sort of malicious and abusive style.

In 1925 the Vakhtangov Theater put on Lidya Seyfullina's *Virineya*, a problem play telling of how the new type of peasant woman is influenced by the revolution.

Leonid Leonov's first play *Untilovsk* was produced at MXAT in 1928. The action took place in a small deserted place in the taiga where some unfortunate people had been brought together by fate. There were many psychological discourses, not much action, and a strong cast. The play ran only for a short time.

In the same year the same theater produced Kataev's *The Embezzlers*. The principal role was played by Tarkhanov, and Toporkov played the role of his factotum Vanechka. What a magnificent pair! There was drunken emotionalism and a typically Russian spirit of "to Hell with everything." Tata Ushakova and I could not tear ourselves away. The play was quickly removed from the repertory.

In the same year, 1928, M.A. and I saw Babel's play *Sunset* at the MXAT 2nd. Old Krik was played by Cheban, his wife Nekhama by Birman, and the son Benya by Bersenev. I remember how indignant M.A. became when Nekhama tells her husband, "And why did they give you a drink, why did they? They gave you a drink of vodka, you mother---- fat mug, you rabid bastard, like a dog."

In 1929 Dostoyevsky's *Uncle's Dream* appeared at MXAT with Khmelev in the main role (I will speak separately about him).

I remember the performance of Shakespeare's *Othello* at the same theater. Othello was played by L.M. Leonidov, Iago by V. Sinitsyn (he later committed suicide), Desdemona by A.K. Tarasova and Cassio by B.N. Livanov. The scenery was painted by the well-known artist Golovin.

M.A. and I were looking forward very much to the opening night. Leonidov was, of course, at least ten years too old for this part. He could no longer play a military leader with flaming passions. Moreover, he kept grabbing on to the scenery as if he were tired, always leaning or resting on it. One of the actors explained to me that he was afraid of heights.

Iago imperceptibly became the central figure, and the spectator's attention was turned to him. Sinitsyn did not present Iago as the classical villain, but simply portrayed a quiet and very insinuating man.

Tarasova looked attractive and sang "Willow" in a moving way. And Cassio (Livanov) was uncommonly handsome, like a picture, against Golovin's luxuriant scenery, showing Renaissance Italy.

We frequently met Vasily Vasilievich Shkvarkin at dress rehearsals and opening nights. He sometimes came to our house with his beautiful wife. He was one of the most educated of all writers. He always conducted himself splendidly. His works were staged—first *A Harmful Element* (1927), then *The Card Sharper* (1929). The greatest success was his comedy *Someone Else's Child*. The public loved to go and see his plays. It was difficult to imagine that this correct and not very easily amused man was able to provoke so much merriment with his comedies.

1930 was a bumper-crop year at MXAT as far as new productions were concerned. *Othello*, Olesha's *Three Fat Men*, Tolstoi's *Resurrection*, and *Advertisement*, a playful and animated translated play in which O.N. Androvskaya shone. The same year MXAT 2nd put on *The Yard*, based on the story of the same title by Anna Karavaeva. I did not see that show. M.A. went alone. When he came home he very amusingly showed with gestures how the hero, a young fellow, spoke: "Here now, I'll take me tooth brush, and I'll go to the boondocks..." Of course, he made all of this up. The line could hardly be said on stage. He told me that in the background a cow was being milked, and hypertrophied sunflowers were swaying in the foreground. He made it all up, but it was amusing.

Along with the problem plays, the news often penetrated into the theater in those years. In this regard the Vakhtangov Theater's production of Yury Slyozkin's play *Fishing* (1931) was particularly characteristic. I no longer remember what the situation was, but it was a year of ration cards.

When the curtain rose, one could see stiff pikes in different poses hanging in a dark fish net (and that particular day one could buy pikes with one's ration cards), and then a soft groan was heard in the theater (the stage designer was N.P Akimov). A team was cleaning fish on stage. And so it was in all three acts—or however many acts there were.

In the summer of 1930 M.A. and I went to the Experimental Theater (on Zimina Street) to hear A.A. Spendiarov's opera *Almast*. The main role was played by Maria Maksakova and Nadir-Shah was played by Alexander Pirogov. This significant and beautiful musical composition ends with a tragic situation. Almast, who has betrayed his Armenian people in the name of honor by opening the gates of the fortress to the Persian conquerors, is led to execution.

When the Spendiarov Theater of Opera and Ballet in Erevan gave *Almast* in Moscow during the Ten Day Festival of Armenian Art in 1969, I did not recognize the finale. Accompanied by cheerful music, young girls in ancient armor filled the stage. They represented Armenian women patriots, introduced into the show to counterbalance the traitorous Almast.

Alexander Spendiarov never wrote anything remotely resembling this. What is happening to the theaters?

I remember once I had the flu with a high fever. When I got out of bed, M.A. suggested that I go with him to the Vakhtangov to see *The Fifth Horizon* (1932, a play by Perets Markish). I didn't know that coal veins are worked by "horizons." I had imagined that *The Fifth Horizon* was on a psychological-philosophical theme. It was terribly dark on the stage. The actor Glazunov stood there in a shiny leather outfit—it seemed that it was dripping wet—wearing some kind of helmet. My head was spinning from my recent fever, and I leaned on M.A.'s shoulder and asked, "Maka, is that a diver?"

"You'd better go home," he said and took me to the cloakroom to get our coats. A friendly writer from the "minor leagues," who was employed at the Vakhtangov Theater, followed us out and whispered, "It wasn't I who wrote it..."

Unfortunately I don't remember the title of the play that ran at the Kamerny Theater. Shaggy and terrible-looking peasants (we said, kulaks) were slinking around the stage, and they were slinking in a special way, all the time turning their profiles to the public as if they were Egyptian frescoes. Then a man from the intelligentsia came in dressed in a well-made suit with a tie and we both said: "the wrecker!" And we were not mistaken. Such standardized types often migrated from one play to another in those days.

There were, of course, interesting shows as well—*The Affair, Eric XIV,* and *The Cricket on the Hearth* with such a star of theatrical arts as Mikhail Chekhov (MXAT 2nd).

Because of its elegance and good ensemble acting I remembered Hamsun's *At the Gates to the Kingdom* for many years. Kachalov was Kareno, S. Elanska was Elina and B.N. Livanov was Bondesen.

We had our own terminology. Gala spectacles which everyone was trying to make seem interesting and colorful with much bustling about and noise, but which remained basically a little boring, we referred to as "good-time boredom" (Lope de Vega, sometimes Shakespeare).

When we ran across something hopelessly antiquated, old-fashioned and comical as well, M.A. called it a "waltz with figures." And this is why. A beginning dramatist once asked Bulgakov to read his play at the Lyamins. It was surprising that when jazz music could be heard all over Europe and when everybody was dancing the one-step and the two-step, the heroes in a contemporary play written by an aspiring playwright danced a "waltz with figures."

And here is the reason why M.A. never actually felt attracted to the movies, although he did write a few scenarios during the course of his life. Sometimes he pretended out of mischief that he did not understand anything in a film. I remember how we were in some movie theater. The programs used to be long and full—a travelogue, the feature, and a newsreel. During the brief intermission he inquired of me with an angelic expression on his face: "Who beat up whom? Did the good guy beat up the bad guy, or the bad guy the good guy?"

I said,"Listen, you, Maka."

And then two nice old ladies assailed me, "Citizeness, if you brought him to the cinematograph (they expressed themselves in such an old-fashioned way), then you must explain everything to the man since he does not understand."

I couldn't tell them that he was a notorious "pretender."

There are two operas that almost seem to accompany Mikhail Bulgakov's work: *Faust* and *Aida*. He remained faithful to them all during his maturity. In the first part of the novel *The White Guard*, *Faust* is mentioned several times. And the "varicolored" red-bearded Valentin sings, "I implore you for my sister's sake." The writer calls this opera the eternal *Faust* and says further that *Faust* is absolutely immortal.

Here is the beginning of the play *Adam and Eve*:

"It is May in Leningrad. A room on the first floor with an open window overlooking the courtyard. Out of the loudspeaker *Faust* pours out sonorously and softly from the Marinsky Theater.

Adam (kissing Eve): Oh, isn't *Faust* a wonderful opera! Do you love me?"

Music is interspersed here and there through Bulgakov's works, but *Aida* is perhaps the most often mentioned. Here is the feuilleton "Forty Times Forty. The Fourth Panorama. Now." (*On the Eve*, No. 310, April 15, 1923). "On the cloth there are waves of light and Radames' triumphal procession comes in waves amidst the clanking of brass and the peals of the choir. In the intermissions the theater gleams in a golden and red light and seems as sumptuously decorated as it used to be."

"My Gods, I pray to you." How many times I heard M.A. hum this aria from *Aida*. In the fantastic tale *Heart of a Dog* the principal character, the surgeon Preobrazhensky, hums

"To the shores of the holy Nile" when he is concentrating very hard. It is an aria from the same opera, and on his rare days of rest he hurries to the Bolshoi Theater to hear *Aida* if it is on. M.A. said, "It is of no importance whatsoever if a work is commissioned or if it was written because the author himself wished to. *Aida* was a commissioned opera, but it turned out remarkably." (Verdi wrote it at the order of the Cairo Opera.) We heard *Aida* together at the Bolshoi.

Music is present in almost all of M.A.'s works. In the story "No. 13, the Elpit-Rabkommun Building," included in the collection *Diaboliad* (1925), the author describes a fire; and suddenly, quite unexpectedly, he changes the comparison of the spreading flames to an intensification of music in an orchestra. "And now not a small prince, but a fiery king started to play a rhapsody quite threateningly. And not *cappriccio*, but terrifyingly—*brioso*."

In *Zoya's Apartment* a sad and languid song by Rakhmaninov is heard: "Do not sing, my beauty, the sad Georgian song to me" M.A. loved to hum this tune, too.

We used to go to concerts. We listened to piano virtuosi— the German Egon Petri and the Italian Carlo Zecchi. I cannot help thinking of M.A.'s words, "Music which helps me to think is specially precious."

We went to the *Persimfans* several times. I will explain for those who do not know what this means—a symphony orchestra without a conductor.

Once when we were at the artists' "Circle" on Pimenovsky Lane—we went there rather frequently—it so happened that we sat down at a table with a pale, polite, and intellectual-looking man. M.A. and he exchanged greetings. We introduced ourselves. He turned out to be the violinist Lev Tsetlin, the first violinist of the *Persimfans*.

"My wife here always gets upset when she hears the *Persimfans*," said M.A.

The musician smiled. "Is it really that awful?"

"It always seems to me that the orchestra members are not going to notice your signs and will not come in on time," said I.

"And are my 'signs,' as you call them, very noticeable?"

"No, not very. That is why I get upset."

M.A. liked to hear the young pianist Petunin play. I remember that one day at the "Circle," we went into the piano room and an attractive young man in a gray suit played some jazz tunes—and he played very well, too.

We had some friends who loved to play music—the artist Mikhail Cheremnykh and his wife Nina. They were a remarkable pair—friendly, pleasant and hospitable. Bulgakov's attitude to Cheremnykh was two-sided; he definitely did not share the artist's enthusiasm for antireligious propaganda (he thought it primitive), but he liked him very much as a person.

Nina would sit down at the instrument. *The Barber of Seville* followed triumphantly: "Soon in the golden east/Dawn will rise all rosy" sang the men in the duet, looking sweetly at each other. Both of them found pleasure in singing, and we enjoyed it too, Nina, her sister Natalya (the most beautiful of all beauties), and I.

It is appropriate to mention here that in his youth M.A. dreamed of becoming a singer. In his early years he kept a photograph of the bass-singer Sibiryakov on his desk; it was inscribed: "Sometimes dreams come true."

M.A.'s acquaintance with the composer Sergei Vasilenko and his family dates from the period of 1929-1930. They were people for every taste—the composer himself, his wife Tatyana, an excellent story teller and a woman with a great sense of humor, Professor Sergei Shambinago (her former husband), an expert on Russian classical literature, and their daughter Elena Kapterova, to whom it was customary to pay court. The family group was completed by the very young Tanya Kapterova and the dog Tuzik.

Singers and musicians were often guests in their home.

In conclusion I would like to mention yet another peculiarity in Bulgakov's works—his taste for the names of famous musicians. In the tale *The Fatal Eggs* there is Rubinstein, the representative of a "certain foreign country" who tried to buy from Professor Persikov the design for the chamber he had invented.

There is Talberg in the novel *The White Guard* and the play *The Days of the Turbins*. Last century the name of the Austrian pianist Sigismond Thalberg was very well-known. It was he who competed with Liszt himself in 1937.

In *The Master and Margarita* the man of letters bears the name of Berlioz. Stravinsky is the name of the psychiatrist in whose care the Master finds himself.

Now I have finally reached the last pages of my memoirs and the last days of our life together in November 1932.

I will not tell about the time of separation which was so difficult for both of us. As a sign of this event I set down a black cross, as is written in the concluding lines of Bulgakov's play *Molière*.

1968–Autumn 1969.